Bridge design for economy and durability

concepts for new, strengthened and replacement bridges

Brian Pritchard, BSc, MS, CEng, FICE, FIHT

 **Thomas Telford, London**

Published by Thomas Telford Services Ltd, Thomas Telford House, 1 Heron Quay, London E14 4JD

First published 1992

A catalogue record for this book is available from the British Library.

ISBN: 0 7277 1671 9

Typeset in Great Britain by Alden Multimedia Ltd.
Printed in Great Britain by Redwood Press Limited, Melksham, Wiltshire

This book is dedicated to my many fellow bridge engineers worldwide

Acknowledgements

The illustrations are taken mainly from the author's work with W.S. Atkins Consultants Ltd. He wishes to thank them and their clients, principally the Department of Transport, for permitting their use. Thanks are also due to the following organisations

Fig. 3.4 courtesy American Portland Cement Association
Fig. 4.9 courtesy MRM Partnership
Fig. 4.12 courtesy Tony Gee + Quandel
Fig. 5.3 courtesy Institution of Structural Engineers
Figs 5.4–5.8 courtesy Transport and Road Research Laboratory
Fig. 7.6 courtesy Lancashire County Council
Figs 7.11 and 9.1 courtesy Gifford & Partners
Figs 10.5 and 10.6 courtesy Kent County Council
Fig. 10.10 courtesy Transport and Road Research Laboratory and Motor Industry Research Association
Figs 11.29–11.31 courtesy SICOM—Sensor & Prestressing Techniques Ltd.
Figs 16.1 and 16.6 courtesy Campenon-Bernard BTP

Thanks are also due to Alan Hayward & Partners who assisted in the design of the viaducts shown in Figs 3.1, 11.19 and 13.2–13.5, and to Taylor Woodrow Construction who provided alternative designs for the flyovers shown in Figs 2.1, 2.3, 4.6–4.8, 7.1, 7.4, 7.5, 7.7 and 8.2.

The author also wishes to thank Alan Whitfield of the Department of Transport for help with the introductions to chapters 15 and 16.

Preface

This book brings together a number of established and new bridge design concepts which were developed during the author's 40 years of close involvement with UK and international bridge consultancy, contracting, code preparation, lecturing and research. The concepts all aim to provide economy and durability in bridging, be it in the design and construction of new bridges or in the additional lifetime operations of the maintenance and possible strengthening or modification due to road widening of existing bridges. The economies are based on fundamental structural relationships and bridge layouts rather than on the relative merits and economies of the two principal construction materials, concrete and steel. In general, the concepts also contribute to good appearance accompanied by ride quality and safety.

The design concepts are conveniently presented in the context of the bridge types most commonly encountered by today's designers. This means highway bridges and viaducts constructed in the small to medium span range of 10–60 m, with an emphasis on decks of reinforced and prestressed concrete or composite steel–concrete appropriate to these spans. Nevertheless, most of the concepts can be applied with advantage to any type or span of bridging.

Chapter 1 describes the various desirable bridge economies, including the economies of durability sought in new design and construction and the economies of minimum traffic disruption sought in any future strengthening or layout changes due to road widening. The design concepts are then presented in five sections

> new superstructures: chapters 2–6
> new substructures: chapters 7–10
> bridge maintenance: chapter 11
> bridge strengthening: chapters 12–14
> bridges for road widening: chapters 15 and 16.

The design concepts cover a wide range of applications: from sucker decks (a new description which one hopes to be appropriate) to inboard piers and from hybrid beams to shock transmission units.

Sucker designs apply deck haunching to suck moments away from critical headroom locations, where minimum deck depth proves beneficial in cost and appearance. Inboard piers are shown to offer considerable economy in urban land take and, when combined with torsionally stiff decks, to allow the square design of skew crossings.

Hybrid prestressed beams also offer economy by combining the quality of factory-produced pre-tensioning with subsequent post-tensioning procedures. Shock transmission units beneficially share out horizontal deck loads due to traction, braking and earthquake among all the bridge supports.

The design concepts in the book are concerned mainly with economy and durability in highway bridging. Bridges are designed to last for at least two human lifespans and it is important that their intrusion on the environment and landscape should be minimal. They should not offend the eye and should age gracefully. A lot of the older arch bridges in the UK appear to fulfil both requirements. Unfortunately, the same cannot always be said about some more recent highway structures.

Good appearance consistent with economy should always be sought by the bridge engineer, and this is where the 'art' of bridge design is so important. This aesthetic skill is difficult to define, but wherever it comes from, and the architect's help should always be welcomed, it must also be allied to technical expertise. Some early bridge-builders even claimed a spiritual influence. The following quotation is taken from a 1944 paper on bridge aesthetics by a past President of the Institution of Civil Engineers, Professor Charles Inglis.

> With the fall of the Roman Empire bridge construction in Europe became almost a lost art; but in the 12th century it was restored by a Benedictine religious order known as Fratres Pontifices. In those days the art of bridge building was regarded as a divine inspiration vouchsafed only to men of exceptional piety, and this may account for the fact that even to this day the official title of the Pope of Rome is Pontifex Maximus, or Bridge Engineer-in-Chief. It certainly accounts for the fact that in many old stone bridges in Great Britain chapels or traces of chapels are to be found incorporated in the structure.

> Most of us will recognise that the exceptional piety is a quality that has not persisted, perhaps today being replaced by the noticeable dedication found in most bridge engineers.

> Moreover, I confess to a feeling that the Pontiff's bridging role really refers to that more important structure between Man and his Diety.

Brian Pritchard, 1992

Contents

Economy and durability in highway bridging: *whole-life cost*

Fig. 1.1. Redbridge Flyover, London

1.1. Whole-life cost

The three decades leading up to the 1980s were marked by massive programmes of motorway and trunk road building in Western Europe and America. Large numbers of bridges were constructed in various combinations of concrete and steel, with the general and comfortable attitude that reinforced concrete and prestressed concrete elements were more durable than structural steel elements and hence economic in terms of lifetime maintenance.

The past decade has indicated a somewhat different picture, as the effects of winter de-icing salt have become painfully evident, leading to extensive reinforcement and tendon corrosion in reinforced and prestressed concrete bridge decks and substructures.[1] Surveys in America estimate that the cost of repair or replacement of such bridges runs into many billions of pounds, and even in the UK a near billion is mentioned.[2] As a result there has been a rapidly increasing awareness of the importance of bridge durability and its effect on the whole-life cost of a bridge.

In addition, the future programme for UK bridges is dominated by two major requirements, costing up to £3000 million in total

(a) to strengthen a large number of existing bridges, principally to cater for the use of 40 t heavy vehicles and 11·5 t axle loads after January 1999, as already permitted in other parts of the European Community
(b) to modify or replace a further large number of existing bridges to accommodate widened motorways and trunk roads.

With the large costs associated with any traffic disruptions caused during strengthening, modification or replacement, a new appreciation has arisen of the need to allow for such possible future operations within the lifetime of a newly designed bridge.

Bridge designers are therefore faced with the idea of whole-life or life-cycle costs, defined as 'the costs of all activities associated with a bridge during its life'. These are relatively new expressions in bridging,[3] where useful life in the UK is currently set at 120 years. In that time-span, the significant cost stages are

(a) the high initial cost of design and construction
(b) the regular inspection and maintenance costs over the bridge lifetime
(c) the repairs which could be expected during the lifetime, costs of which include those relating to traffic disruption
(d) the possibility of one or more strengthening operations to cater for increased traffic loading or design code changes, with again the costs of possible traffic disruption
(e) the possibility of bridge modification or replacement on-line due to widening of the road carried or crossed, with even greater costs of possible traffic disruption.

It follows that bridge economy must be considered as whole-life, and any cost comparisons used by the bridge engineer at initial design stage must go beyond the estimated initial design and construction costs. Also included must be the estimated costs of planned lifetime inspection and maintenance operations,[4] with commuted costs used to assist in the choice between, say, frequent low-cost operations and infrequent more expensive operations. Some cost comparisons should also be added for the relative ease and economies of any future repairs, strengthening, or modifications or replacements arising from road widening.

The economies which are the most significant to the various lifetime stages defined are described in the following sections.

1.2. Design and construction economy

The aspiring bridge engineer seeks to design new highway bridges which will incorporate the following desirable features

(a)   design and construction economy in both time and money
(b)   good appearance
(c)   ride quality and safety
(d)   ease of access for inspection and maintenance
(e)   a design life of at least 120 years in the UK, with a minimum of maintenance
(f)   ready repeatability and standardisation for multi-span or multi-bridge applications
(g)   ease of repair, possible strengthening and possible modification or replacement during road widening.

Good design practice always produces several initial designs using different span arrangements and various relevant construction materials and techniques. After an initial 'coarse sieving' of the differing proposals, using judgments based on the desirable features listed above, the choice is ideally reduced to two alternatives. A 'finer sieving' procedure will usually produce a preferred alternative, which can then be recommended to the client.

In such a procedure it is clear that different weightings can be placed on each of the desirable features. In most instances, however, the high first cost of construction tends to dominate the choice between alternatives, with the estimated periodic costs of maintenance, and ease of access, repair, and strengthening, modification or replacement only recently gaining importance in the overall cost considerations.

The principal choice in the UK for bridges and flyovers of short to medium span has always been a keen contest between structural steel and concrete for the deck. Over the years the relative construction costs have fluctuated to marginally favour one or the other.

Fig. 1.2. Redbridge Flyover and approach ramp

Very often the designer is faced with steel and concrete alternatives which have both fulfilled his requirements, but which are separated only by these marginal cost differences, which could perhaps reverse in the period between design choice and actual tender and construction.

In recent UK practice there have been several instances of important flyovers designed and put to tender using fully designed and documented steel and concrete alternatives. The Redbridge Flyover built recently in North London (Figs 1.1 and 1.2) was a case where the prestressed concrete box girder alternative was priced marginally lower than the composite steel girder/ concrete deck slab alternative, and built.

There have been even more examples of alternative designs produced by tenderers being accepted and built in place of the original design.[5] In these instances, it is generally the steel composite structure which replaces the original prestressed concrete design.

Thus it can be said that for typical new highway bridges of short to medium span in the UK, economic choices at design stage based on design and construction cost are only marginally affected by the construction materials and method. It is the purpose of this book to demonstrate that more fundamental choices about the arrangement and shape of the bridge offer the possibility of more significant economies, both in the high initial first cost and the continuing cost of maintenance and possible strengthening, modification or replacement.

For instance, the deck of the Redbridge Flyover shown in Figs 1.1 and 1.2 was marginally cheaper at tender using prestressed concrete rather than composite steel/concrete construction. However, greater cost savings were derived from the decision to make the deck continuous rather than simply supported. Not only was the viaduct structure itself cheaper, due to savings in the deck construction depth and the substructure, but also the depth saving reduced the maximum height and total length of the approach ramps, providing more savings. Continuity and associated savings in deck construction depth always offer such economy, and the six chapters listed under the general heading of 'New superstructures' elaborate on these matters: chapter 2 describes the advantages to be gained from general bridge deck continuity; chapter 3 shows how locally to minimise deck construction depths at critical headroom locations by constructing variable depth decks; chapter 4 demonstrates how most of the advantages of continuity of variable depth decks can be added to single-span bridges by counterweighting or to viaducts by using cantilever construction; chapter 5 introduces the advantages to be gained by adding continuity to the factory qualities of precast pre-tensioned beams; and chapter 6 adds further advantage to precast beam continuity by using hybrid post-tensioned and pre-tensioned beams rather than draped pre-tensioning strand beams.

Bridge substructures, defined as support piers and abutments plus associated foundations, do not always receive the same attention during design as the bridge deck. This is partly due to the fact that nearly all substructures are constructed of in situ reinforced concrete and the keen competition between structural steelwork and concrete, very much present in deck design, is just not there.

With piled substructures sometimes approaching the cost of the deck supported, it is obviously desirable to consider the economy of substructures by going through a shortened version of the sieving procedure described earlier, applied to the desirable features required in substructures. Cost of construction will be partly dependent on the type of deck carried, and here the weight saved by using steel deck construction can be significant where the ground is poor. Nevertheless, several design concepts can be used to add

Fig. 1.3. Durability of simply supported viaduct

further economy and these are described in four chapters under the general heading 'New substructures': chapter 7 shows how the adoption of inboard piers (i.e. with overhang decks) can reduce ground intrusion, save land and housing demolition in urban situations and simplify skew problems; chapter 8 describes how significant cost savings can be made by minimising the restraints offered by the substructures to the articulation of the deck carried (i.e. the deck movements principally due to thermal, shrinkage and creep effects); chapter 9 describes the optimum and most economic articulation of plan-curved bridges; and chapter 10 details the uses of substructure-mounted shock transmission units (STUs) for beneficially sharing out horizontal traction, braking and earthquake loading.

1.3. Durability and maintenance economy

The durability of the newly designed and constructed bridge and the resulting economy of maintenance is generally the second most important component of the whole-life cost. Indeed, it is encouraging to note more discrimination, particularly with clients, into the benefits of paying extra in first cost for a more durable bridge.

Deck continuity and the minimising of deck joints is undoubtedly one of the key factors contributing to the durability and ease of maintenance of both bridge decks and substructures. This is very evident in comparing the relative damage due to winter de-icing salt between the simply supported flyover of Fig. 1.3 and the continuous flyover of about the same age shown in Fig. 2.1.

Under the heading 'Bridge maintenance', chapter 11 shows how bridges can be designed to offer minimum maintenance by maximising their resistance to the most harmful cause of deterioration—corrosion due to winter de-icing salt.

1.4. Strengthening economy

With a more than possible chance that the newly designed bridge will require some strengthening during its lifetime, a careful engineer and client will make some effort to ensure that such strengthening can be undertaken with economy. Such economy is usually dominated by one factor—the cost of disrupting or even stopping the traffic flow on or below the bridge during strengthening.

It has been suggested that bridge decks should be designed as a number of longitudinal beams each supporting one lane of traffic, thus simplifying the lane closures required for piecemeal repair or reconstruction.[6] However, this still means that the high costs of temporary lane closures and irritation to the road user remain.

Under the heading 'Bridge strengthening', three chapters describe methods of strengthening which can be tailored to require few, if any, lane closures and little interference with traffic: chapter 12 describes post-tensioning and load-sharing procedures which can be used to strengthen steel composite decks, reinforced concrete decks and arches; chapter 13 introduces the drilled-in tension pin shear connector for strengthening and improving the fatigue lives of steel–concrete composite decks; and chapter 14 shows how to relieve under-strength bridge substructures by horizontal load sharing using STUs.

1.5. Road-widening economy

Under the heading 'Bridges for road widening', two chapters describe methods of underbridge widening and overbridge lengthening required by road widening; in these methods, extra disruption of traffic is kept to a minimum: chapter 15 describes the modification of existing bridges, and chapter 16 describes bridge replacements.

1.6. References

1. PRITCHARD. Road salt corrosion in UK concrete bridges. *Construction Repair*, 1986, Sept., Nov.
2. WALLBANK. *The performance of concrete in bridges: a survey of 200 highway bridges*. HMSO, London, 1989.
3. GORDON. Durability of highway bridges. IABSE symposium, Lisbon, 1989.
4. DEPARTMENT OF TRANSPORT. *Evaluation of maintenance costs in comparing alternative designs for highway structures*. HMSO, London, 1988, DTp Departmental Advice Note BA28/88.
5. HAYWARD. State of the art highway bridges. ECCS/BCSA international symposium on steel bridges, London, 1988.
6. SIMPSON *et al*. Design for reconstruction and maintainability. IABSE symposium, Paris, 1987.

2

Advantages of deck continuity:
minimising deck depths, joints, bearings and maintenance

2.1. Deck continuity
2.2. Advantages
2.3. Savings in deck construction depth
2.4. References

Fig. 2.1. A5 flyover, Staples Corner Interchange, London

2.1. Deck continuity

Early multi-span beam and slab or slab bridges were generally designed and built as a sequence of simply supported spans. In 1930 the American, Hardy Cross, introduced his famous moment distribution method for the quick and easy analysis of continuous frames and beams.[1] This method was immediately taken on by bridge designers and a gradual build-up in the use of deck continuity commenced.

The 1950s and 1960s saw a further great improvement in continuous-deck analysis with the introduction of computers, together with grillage and finite element programs. The use of continuity spread, particularly in winter-affected countries where the maintenance problems of deck joints and de-icing salt have dramatically multiplied. In some countries national bridge codes recommend or even dictate multi-span deck continuity unless ground settlement problems require the greater articulation provided by a series of simply supported spans.

Currently, the Department of Transport (DTp) is considering the issue of an advice note encouraging bridge designers to use deck continuity, principally to minimise the use of trouble-prone deck joints. Included will be further recommendations on methods of providing continuity for the most common deck form—precast pre-tensioned concrete beams supporting, and composite with, reinforced concrete deck slabs. This latter recommendation is treated in chapter 5.

A lot of world-wide interest is being shown in 'integral bridges', in which the continuity of bridge decks free of intermediate joints is extended to the elimination of the end expansion joints by building the deck into the abutments.[2]

The elimination of deck joints is a good and sufficient reason for adopting deck continuity, with all the implied savings in maintenance costs, and this is dealt with in chapter 11. However, it should be remembered that deck continuity can also offer considerable economies in first-time construction costs. It is this aspect which is emphasised in sections 2.2 and 2.3.

Continuity can be adopted for most multi-span bridges. Only in very short span structures and in mining areas will differential pier and abutment settlements become significant enough to dictate a change to simply supported spans.

Differential settlements in highway bridges rarely exceed 10–20 mm and in the more critical shorter spans there is a tendency to use reinforced concrete decks anyway. Because of the lower concrete elasticity modulus and inherent cracking, reinforced concrete is less stiff than prestressed concrete and accommodates differential settlement with less attracted moment.

In certain cases single-span or three-span decks subject to significant settlements can be given some of the benefits of continuity by counterweighting (see chapter 4).

2.2. Advantages

Figure 2.2 illustrates the main advantages to be gained by using multi-span deck continuity: part (a) shows a typical simply supported multi-span deck, part (b) a corresponding continuous deck.

The first advantage is the elimination of deck and parapet joints at the piers. This represents savings in both construction and maintenance costs—maintenance which includes that of the underlying piers (see sections 11.3 and 11.4). Elimination of joints also gives the vehicles crossing the bridge a better ride.

The second advantage is the saving in deck depth, which not only can reduce the construction cost of both the deck and the supporting substructure but also can reduce the cost of associated approach ramps or earthworks. The

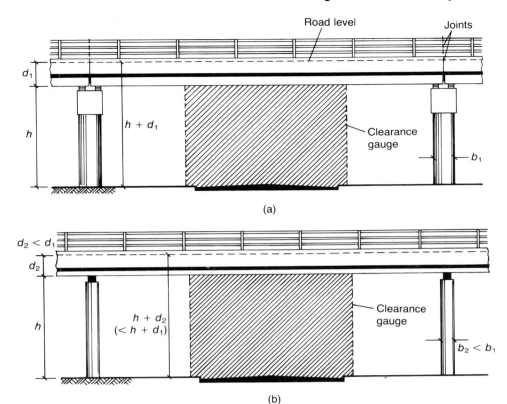

Fig. 2.2. Advantages of continuity: (a) simply supported deck; (b) continuous deck

latter saving is probably the most significant construction-cost economy and is dealt with separately in section 2.3.

The third advantage lies in the halving of the number of bearings required at each pier. Although the bearings will be of higher capacity, the lesser number should result in cost savings.

The fourth advantage results from the replacement of the two rows of bearings by the single row of central bearings. The piers or crossheads can be reduced in thickness not only because the single row of bearings takes up less room at the top, but because the deck dead load has reduced and the live load moments applied by off-centre pairs of bearings are removed. Significant cost savings in pier foundations also result.

A fifth advantage, possible only with deck continuity, is that the 'sucker deck' principle, covered in the next chapter, can be applied to advantage.

A sixth advantage, again possible only with deck continuity, is that single bearing supports, covered in chapter 7, can also be applied to advantage.

A seventh advantage is that continuity means extra deck redundancy, which generally guards against sudden collapse in overload situations or in instances of sabotage (Fig. 2.3).

2.3. Savings in deck construction depth

The optimum construction depth/span ratios vary with span, live loading, materials and methods of construction. Average ratios for the 10–60 m span range considered in this book are about 1/24 for continuous spans and 1/18 for simply supported spans. Thus, for 35–40 m spans about a half metre can be saved in deck construction depth by adopting continuity. In itself, the reduction in concrete or steel would appear to lead to a reduction in construction cost. This is not always the case, as continuity can introduce extra

Fig. 2.3. Bomb damage to A5 flyover, Staples Corner Interchange

Fig. 2.4. Approach ramp savings: (a) simply supported spans; (b) continuous spans

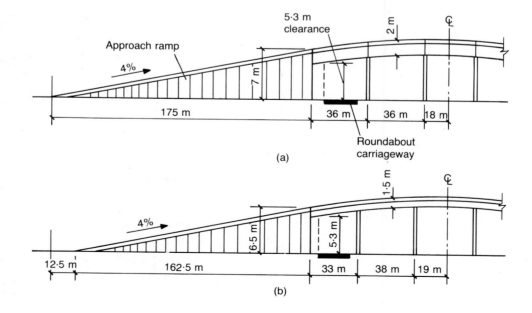

complications to the sequence and standardisation of construction, usually more perceived than real if design and construction is adequately planned to suit the continuity.

Whether the continuous deck is cheaper to build or not, the associated saving in construction depth can certainly reduce construction costs of other elements of the bridge or viaduct. The substructure, of course, can benefit by reductions of up to 10–15% in deck weight, significant with the longer spans and where foundations are poor. However, it is the possible reductions in related earthworks, approach ramps or bridge lengths which are most cost-effective. Typical examples are demonstrated in Figs 2.4–2.6.

Figure 2.4 shows a typical urban flyover carrying a highway over a ground-level roundabout. The approach ramps rise at a 4% grade and the 180 m long viaduct has a compliant vertical curve providing the required headroom over the underlying roundabout carriageways. In part (a) of the figure there are five equal 36 m simply supported spans with a deck construction depth of 2 m. The resulting maximum ramp height is 7 m, giving an overall length of 175 m for each ramp.

The proposal in part (b) of Fig. 2.4 uses span continuity and slightly modifies the span layouts to give the more balanced arrangement of shorter end spans. This results in three inner spans of 38 m and two end spans of 33 m. The associated reduction in deck depth of 0·5 m means that the maximum ramp height drops to 6·5 m and the ramp length reduces to 162·5 m.

The total reduction in the approach ramps due to the introduction of viaduct continuity is therefore measured by a 7% reduction in length and height. This results in a reduction of nearly 14% in ramp wall area, which also gives a rough approximation of the cost saving in ramp construction at each end. Fig. 2.5 shows an early flyover over the M1 which benefited with

Fig. 2.5. M1 flyover, Hendon Fiveways Interchange, London

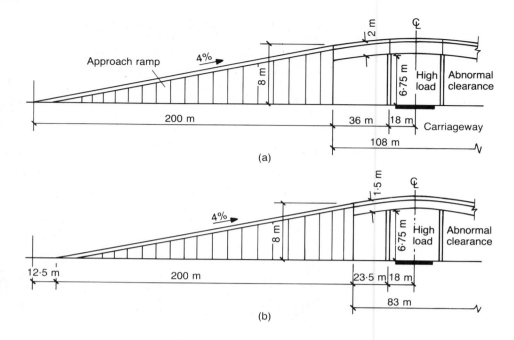

Fig. 2.6. Savings in flyover length: (a) simply supported spans; (b) continuous spans

significant ramp savings generated by the depth reduction in the continuous decks.

Figure 2.6 shows another flyover with a similar vertical profile, this time crossing a centrally located urban carriageway flanked by pedestrian areas. In this case, the designer again chooses to use approach ramps rather than embankments to reduce landtake. His calculations show that the ramps can rise to a height of 8 m using spread footings for the ramp walls, while remaining cheaper per square metre than suspended deck. Anything higher would require expensive piling, exceeding the cost of suspended deck. The maximum length of each of the 4% ramps is therefore set at 200 m.

A 36 m span is required across the central carriageway and part (a) of Fig. 2.6 shows a sequence of three equal 36 m simply supported spans, the outer spans crossing the paved pedestrian areas. The 2 m deck construction depth results in the maximum allowable ramp height of 8 m and length of 200 m.

Part (b) of Fig. 2.6 shows the effect of providing span continuity and the associated 0·5 m saving in deck construction depth. The 200 m long, 8 m high ramps are retained, but each can now be relocated 12·5 m nearer the central

Fig. 2.7. Excavation savings, depressed motorway

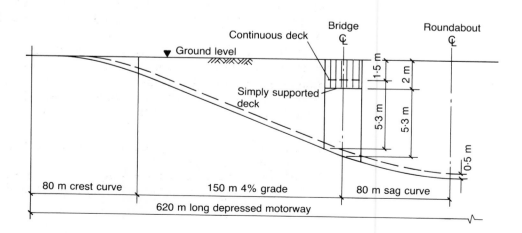

Fig. 2.8. Depressed M25 Interchange

carriageway, reducing the required viaduct length from 108 m to 83 m and the end spans from 36 m to 23·5 m. Thus, with a probably unimportant small loss of pedestrian area and no change in the approach ramps, the flyover viaduct length is reduced by some 24%, with similar percentage savings in viaduct cost and, possibly, landtake.

The final example, shown in Fig. 2.7, is a dual three-lane motorway locally depressed to pass under twin 36 m span simply supported bridges carrying a 160 m dia. ground level roundabout. In this case the vertical profile of the motorway consists of an 80 m long crest curve followed by a 4% downgrade section 150 m long, then a sag curve 160 m long followed by 150 m of 4% upgrade and a final 80 m long crest curve. The bridges are located just above the ends of the sag curve, which are 7·3 m below ground level. This depth provides the required 5·3 m clearance under the 2 m deck construction depth.

The depressed section of motorway is 620 m long and the excavation required with 1 : 2 cutting slopes will be around 150 000 m³. Savings can be made by adding continuity to the roundabout bridge decks. The 0·5 m deck construction depth saved allows the depressed motorway profile to be raised by the same amount, shown as a broken line on the figure. This saves approximately 15 000 m³, or 10%, of the excavation. There are also small savings in land aquisition and, indeed, in the overall length of the roundabout overbridges.

Depending on the excavated material and its ease of disposal, the excavation cost savings which result from changing the roundabout bridge deck from simply supported to continuous can readily exceed £100 000. In rock, of course, the saving could be many times higher. Fig. 2.8 shows such a depressed interchange, in this case with an additional top-layer flyover.

2.4. References

1. CROSS. Analysis of continuous frames by distributing fixed-end moments. *Proc. Am. Soc. Civ. Engrs*, 1930.
2. BURKE. The integrated construction and conversion of single and multispan bridges. Bridge Management International Symposium, Surrey University, 1990.

Sucker decks: *minimising deck depths at critical headroom locations*

Fig. 3.1. Flyover, Stoke-on-Trent

3.1. The sucker deck principle

Early in my career I was fortunate enough to find myself working in Copenhagen for a gifted Danish bridge engineer. Among other design concepts, he introduced me to the advantages of variable depth bridge deck construction (Figs 3.1 and 3.2).

With a memorable turn of phrase he explained that the increased depth of construction, or haunching, at the supports of a multi-span continuous deck 'sucked' sagging moments away from the midspan regions by increasing the hogging moments over the supports. The degree of suction increased with the stiffness differential arising from the haunching. This is illustrated in Fig. 3.3, where a slab deck is parabolically haunched between fixed supports at A and B, the degree of haunching represented by a depth reduction of kd at midspan from depths d at the supports. Bending moments are shown for applied uniform loading for values of k ranging between 0 and 1, the table giving moments and stresses at A, B and midspan AB.

The typical bending of a deck of uniform depth is shown by the lowest curve, with $k = 0$, for which support and midspan moments have the conventional values of $-0.0833wL^2$ and $+0.0417wL^2$. As k increases so does the moment-sucking effect. At $k = 0.5$ the support moment increases to $-0.1025wL^2$ and the midspan moment decreases to $+0.0225wL^2$. It is also seen that, despite the large depth reduction, the midspan bending stresses are less than at the supports and little more than the maximum stresses in the uniform depth deck. The 23% increase in the support stresses is normally offset by the considerable reduction in self-weight stresses and in stresses benefiting from the stiffness reductions, such as differential temperature, shrinkage and settlement.

With the lower-bound moment curve represented by the uniform-depth deck with $k = 0$, the upper-bound curve is given by $k = 1$. This means zero depth at midspan and results in an idealised pair of pin-connected cantilevers, with moment values of $-0.125wL^2$ at the supports and zero at midspan. All moments for sucker bridges with this type of end fixity, loading and deck soffit shaping lie between these bounds, and similar bodies of moment curves can be drawn up for all the loading conditions and for differing soffit shapes. It should be remembered that these upper-bound and lower-bound cases are not in themselves sucker decks.

The important advantage offered by the concept, labelled thereafter as the 'sucker deck principle', was that continuous multi-span bridge decks could be suitably haunched to produce deck depths at critical headroom locations, usually midspan, less than would be required for a uniform depth deck. The economies of construction-depth saving achieved by adding continuity to constant depth decks, described in chapter 2, can thus be extended by further localised depth savings arising from the variable depths associated with sucker decks.

Fig. 3.2. Sucker deck arrangements

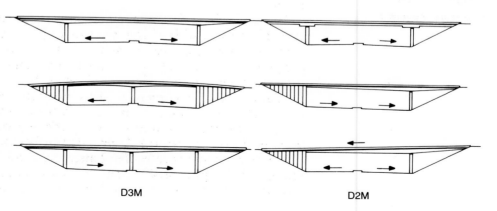

D3M   D2M

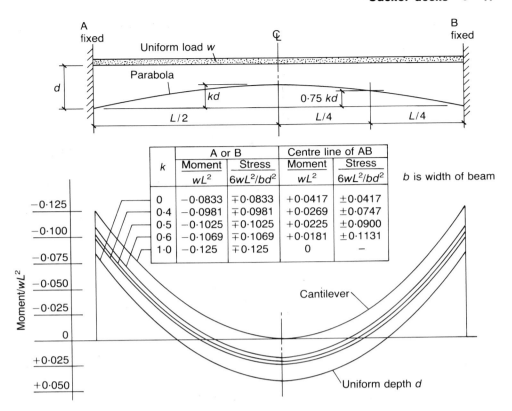

Fig. 3.3. Moment suction from midspan to support

These further savings are created by locating the minimum depth of the sucker deck over the highest point on the headroom clearance diagram of the underlying carriageway, railway, river, canal or local obstacle crossed by the sucker deck.

In the rest of this chapter, after a demonstration of the moment and stress savings associated with sucker decks and a description of various clearance diagrams required for bridges, it is shown how an appropriate form of sucker deck can be fashioned for each type of clearance to effect these extra savings in deck depth to advantage. The further benefits of a safer method of weight-saving than deck-voiding and the aesthetic gains possible are also discussed.

3.2. Bending moments and stresses in sucker decks

The haunches which give rise to the moment-suction effects in continuous decks are always located over a support pier. As shown in Fig. 3.2, they may be localised or over a full span length, stepped, straight-tapered, circular or parabolic.

The analysis and design of these types of deck is nowadays relatively straightforward, with a large number of plane and three-dimensional frame computer programs readily available to the engineer. Nevertheless, initial design can be undertaken in a quick and simple set of moment-distribution procedures based on a very useful set of tables published by the American Portland Cement Association.[1] This puts together in tabular form the carry-over and stiffness factors together with fixed-end moment coefficients for uniform, concentrated and haunch loads applied to deck slabs or beams of variable depth (and width). A typical page from the tables is shown in Fig. 3.4.

Figure 3.5 demonstrates the changes in bending moments and stresses in a reinforced or prestressed concrete slab deck, most commonly used in motorway overbridges, with and without haunching, with the typical suction

Parabolic Haunches — Constant Width

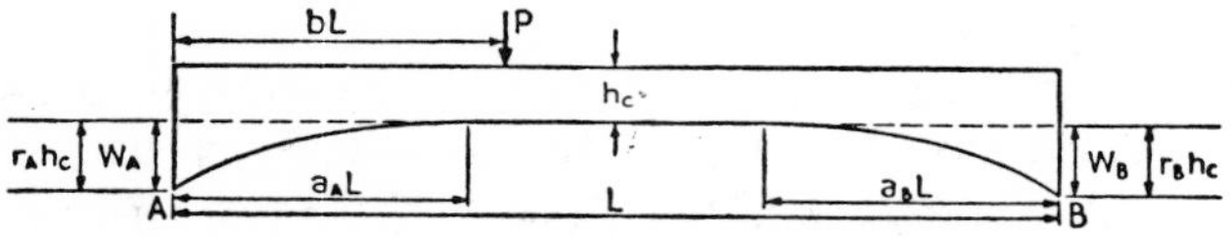

Note:

All carry-over factors and fixed end moment coefficients are negative and all stiffness factors are positive.

Right Haunch		Carry-over Factors		Stiffness Factors		Unif. Load F.E.M. Coef. × wL^2		Concentrated Load F.E.M.—Coef. × PL										Haunch Load at			
								b										Left		Right	
								0.1		0.3		0.5		0.7		0.9		F.E.M. Coef. × $W_A L^2$		F.E.M. Coef. × $W_B L^2$	
a_B	r_B	C_{AB}	C_{BA}	k_{AB}	k_{BA}	M_{AB}	M_{BA}	M_{AB}	M_{BA}	M_{AB}	M_{BA}	M_{AB}	M_{BA}	M_{AB}	M_{BA}	M_{AB}	M_{BA}	M_{AB}	M_{BA}	M_{AB}	M_{BA}
$a_A = 0.5$				a_B = variable						TABLE 25					$r_A = 2.0$				r_B = variable		
0.1	0.4	0.439	1.003	14.05	6.05	0.1524	0.0590	0.0967	0.0014	0.2493	0.0195	0.2667	0.0745	0.1411	0.1263	0.0159	0.0831	0.0187	0.0008	0.0000	0.0008
	0.6	0.445	1.001	14.25	6.30	0.1498	0.0610	0.0967	0.0014	0.2486	0.0205	0.2640	0.0775	0.1368	0.1311	0.0136	0.0855	0.0187	0.0009	0.0000	0.0008
	1.0	0.453	0.999	14.60	6.60	0.1470	0.0640	0.0967	0.0015	0.2474	0.0219	0.2593	0.0819	0.1304	0.1374	0.0104	0.0887	0.0187	0.0009	0.0000	0.0008
	1.5	0.462	0.998	14.90	6.90	0.1448	0.0670	0.0967	0.0015	0.2460	0.0228	0.2559	0.0857	0.1245	0.1428	0.0080	0.0912	0.0186	0.0010	0.0000	0.0008
	2.0	0.470	0.997	15.20	7.19	0.1430	0.0684	0.0967	0.0016	0.2442	0.0232	0.2533	0.0885	0.1209	0.1472	0.0065	0.0929	0.0185	0.0011	0.0000	0.0008
0.2	0.4	0.456	0.989	14.65	6.74	0.1483	0.0632	0.0967	0.0015	0.2472	0.0213	0.2601	0.0819	0.1314	0.1369	0.0144	0.0849	0.0186	0.0009	0.0003	0.0029
	0.6	0.478	0.981	15.05	7.30	0.1440	0.0678	0.0967	0.0016	0.2461	0.0235	0.2544	0.0879	0.1234	0.1461	0.0113	Q.0878	0.0186	0.0010	0.0003	0.0030
	1.0	0.507	0.970	15.80	8.23	0.1386	0.0736	0.0966	0.0018	0.2435	0.0263	0.2453	0.0978	0.1098	0.1604	0.0077	0.0917	0.0185	0.0011	0.0002	0.0031
	1.5	0.529	0.963	16.60	9.15	0.1340	0.0793	0.0965	0.0019	0.2407	0.0289	0.2375	0.1069	0.0987	0.1733	0.0049	0.0945	0.0184	0.0012	0.0001	0.0032
	2.0	0.548	0.960	17.20	9.81	0.1302	0.0827	0.0963	0.0020	0.2384	0.0304	0.2315	0.1135	0.0908	0.1822	0.0034	0.0963	0.0183	0.0013	0.0001	0.0032
0.3	0.4	0.479	0.970	15.08	7.43	0.1457	0.0660	0.0966	0.0016	0.2460	0.0231	0.2554	0.0879	0.1258	0.1433	0.0143	0.0847	0.0186	0.0009	0.0014	0.0060
	0.6	0.512	0.957	15.65	8.40	0.1405	0.0716	0.0966	0.0018	0.2440	0.0261	0.2473	0.0966	0.1146	0.1559	0.0114	0.0875	0.0185	0.0011	0.0010	0.0063
	1.0	0.560	0.938	16.90	10.15	0.1329	0.0803	0.0963	0.0021	0.2399	0.0306	0.2339	0.1122	0.0968	0.1760	0.0076	0.0915	0.0184	0.0013	0.0008	0.0066
	1.5	0.598	0.920	18.20	11.90	0.1263	0.0898	0.0961	0.0025	0.2359	0.0353	0.2212	0.1275	0.0807	0.1955	0.0048	0.0944	0.0182	0.0014	0.0005	0.0068
	2.0	0.629	0.910	19.20	13.35	0.1208	0.0949	0.0958	0.0027	0.2328	0.0384	0.2112	0.1395	0.0689	0.2092	0.0033	0.0962	0.0181	0.0016	0.0004	0.0070
0.4	0.4	0.499	0.947	15.40	8.08	0.1443	0.0674	0.0965	0.0017	0.2448	0.0244	0.2522	0.0913	0.1229	0.1456	0.0145	0.0841	0.0186	0.0010	0.0031	0.0098
	0.6	0.541	0.926	16.30	9.48	0.1388	0.0738	0.0964	0.0019	0.2420	0.0283	0.2425	0.1027	0.1105	0.1590	0.0118	0.0867	0.0185	0.0012	0.0025	0.0102
	1.0	0.606	0.895	17.90	12.10	0.1295	0.0847	0.0960	0.0024	0.2371	0.0346	0.2251	0.1233	0.0906	0.1823	0.0079	0.0907	0.0183	0.0014	0.0018	0.0111
	1.5	0.661	0.868	19.70	15.05	0.1212	0.0961	0.0957	0.0029	0.2316	0.0414	0.2081	0.1452	0.0720	0.2047	0.0052	0.0937	0.0180	0.0016	0.0015	0.0116
	2.0	0.707	0.851	21.20	17.65	0.1142	0.1040	0.0953	0.0034	0.2275	0.0469	0.1940	0.1637	0.0584	0.2212	0.0037	0.0955	0.0178	0.0019	0.0011	0.0120
0.5	0.4	0.513	0.924	15.59	8.67	0.1436	0.0682	0.0964	0.0018	0.2441	0.0256	0.2499	0.0933	0.1217	0.1449	0.0147	0.0835	0.0185	0.0011	0.0057	0.0138
	0.6	0.562	0.894	16.62	10.45	0.1376	0.0750	0.0961	0.0021	0.2408	0.0297	0.2388	0.1064	0.1084	0.1591	0.0120	0.0861	0.0184	0.0013	0.0050	0.0145
	1.0	0.642	0.850	18.64	14.09	0.1275	0.0870	0.0957	0.0027	0.2348	0.0376	0.2193	0.1307	0.0877	0.1825	0.0082	0.0901	0.0181	0.0016	0.0039	0.0157
	1.5	0.721	0.812	20.89	18.60	0.1176	0.0995	0.0952	0.0034	0.2282	0.0466	0.1988	0.1578	0.0687	0.2052	0.0057	0.0928	0.0178	0.0020	0.0030	0.0168
	2.0	0.784	0.784	22.83	22.83	0.1099	0.1099	0.0947	0.0040	0.2224	0.0549	0.1816	0.1816	0.0549	0.2224	0.0040	0.0947	0.0176	0.0023	0.0023	0.0176
$a_A = 0$				a_B = variable						TABLE 26					$r_A = 0$				r_B = variable		
0.1	0.4	0.539	0.498	4.10	4.44	0.0795	0.0914	0.0806	0.0100	0.1439	0.0696	0.1189	0.1378	0.0561	0.1614	0.0060	0.0872	0.0000	0.0000	0.0000	0.0008
	0.6	0.551	0.497	4.13	4.59	0.0782	0.0940	0.0804	0.0103	0.1429	0.0717	0.1169	0.1419	0.0539	0.1660	0.0051	0.0891	0.0000	0.0000	0.0000	0.0008
	1.0	0.569	0.496	4.18	4.79	0.0765	0.0976	0.0802	0.0107	0.1414	0.0747	0.1141	0.1478	0.0508	0.1726	0.0039	0.0917	0.0000	0.0000	0.0000	0.0008
	1.5	0.583	0.495	4.22	4.97	0.0751	0.1007	0.0800	0.0111	0.1402	0.0772	0.1119	0.1527	0.0483	0.1779	0.0030	0.0936	0.0000	0.0000	0.0000	0.0008
	2.0	0.593	0.494	4.24	5.09	0.0742	0.1026	0.0799	0.0113	0.1394	0.0790	0.1103	0.1560	0.0466	0.1816	0.0024	0.0948	0.0000	0.0000	0.0000	0.0008
0.2	0.4	0.575	0.492	4.19	4.89	0.0768	0.0975	0.0802	0.0108	0.1413	0.0754	0.1141	0.1487	0.0513	0.1724	0.0052	0.0888	0.0000	0.0000	0.0001	0.0030
	0.6	0.600	0.489	4.25	5.22	0.0745	0.1025	0.0799	0.0115	0.1393	0.0799	0.1103	0.1572	0.0472	0.1812	0.0041	0.0912	0.0000	0.0000	0.0001	0.0031
	1.0	0.638	0.485	4.35	5.72	0.0712	0.1098	0.0794	0.0125	0.1363	0.0867	0.1046	0.1699	0.0413	0.1943	0.0027	0.0942	0.0000	0.0000	0.0001	0.0032
	1.5	0.670	0.482	4.44	6.17	0.0684	0.1162	0.0791	0.0133	0.1337	0.0926	0.0997	0.1810	0.0364	0.2054	0.0017	0.0963	0.0000	0.0000	0.0000	0.0032
	2.0	0.692	0.479	4.50	6.50	0.0665	0.1205	0.0788	0.0140	0.1318	0.0968	0.0963	0.1889	0.0331	0.2132	0.0012	0.0975	0.0000	0.0000	0.0000	0.0033
0.3	0.4	0.606	0.483	4.25	5.33	0.0750	0.1018	0.0799	0.0116	0.1393	0.0804	0.1106	0.1574	0.0483	0.1793	0.0051	0.0889	0.0000	0.0000	0.0005	0.0064
	0.6	0.645	0.478	4.35	5.88	0.0720	0.1088	0.0794	0.0126	0.1364	0.0872	0.1052	0.1700	0.0430	0.1913	0.0040	0.0912	0.0000	0.0000	0.0004	0.0066
	1.0	0.705	0.469	4.51	6.77	0.0673	0.1196	0.0787	0.0142	0.1318	0.0982	0.0967	0.1899	0.0351	0.2097	0.0027	0.0942	0.0000	0.0000	0.0003	0.0069
	1.5	0.758	0.462	4.65	7.64	0.0633	0.1293	0.0781	0.0158	0.1276	0.1085	0.0892	0.2082	0.0283	0.2258	0.0016	0.0964	0.0000	0.0000	0.0002	0.0071
	2.0	0.797	0.456	4.75	8.30	0.0605	0.1362	0.0777	0.0169	0.1245	0.1161	0.0837	0.2218	0.0236	0.2372	0.0011	0.0976	0.0000	0.0000	0.0001	0.0072
0.4	0.4	0.632	0.473	4.31	5.76	0.0739	0.1045	0.0797	0.0122	0.1379	0.0844	0.1082	0.1636	0.0468	0.1823	0.0052	0.0885	0.0000	0.0000	0.0011	0.0107
	0.6	0.684	0.463	4.43	6.54	0.0703	0.1129	0.0791	0.0136	0.1342	0.0934	0.1016	0.1795	0.0409	0.1958	0.0041	0.0908	0.0000	0.0000	0.0009	0.0111
	1.0	0.768	0.450	4.64	7.93	0.0647	0.1266	0.0781	0.0159	0.1280	0.1086	0.0907	0.2060	0.0319	0.2169	0.0027	0.0939	0.0000	0.0000	0.0006	0.0119
	1.5	0.847	0.438	4.84	9.37	0.0596	0.1395	0.0773	0.0183	0.1223	0.1239	0.0808	0.2319	0.0242	0.2357	0.0017	0.0961	0.0000	0.0000	0.0005	0.0122
	2.0	0.905	0.429	5.00	10.55	0.0559	0.1491	0.0766	0.0201	0.1178	0.1359	0.0733	0.2519	0.0190	0.2489	0.0011	0.0973	0.0000	0.0000	0.0003	0.0125
0.5	0.4	0.653	0.461	4.34	6.16	0.0732	0.1058	0.0794	0.0127	0.1368	0.0873	0.1066	0.1672	0.0463	0.1823	0.0053	0.0877	0.0000	0.0000	0.0021	0.0155
	0.6	0.717	0.448	4.48	7.21	0.0693	0.1151	0.0788	0.0144	0.1325	0.0980	0.0991	0.1855	0.0399	0.1963	0.0042	0.0903	0.0000	0.0000	0.0018	0.0162
	1.0	0.824	0.428	4.75	9.12	0.0628	0.1310	0.0777	0.0174	0.1252	0.1173	0.0866	0.2171	0.0306	0.2181	0.0027	0.0933	0.0000	0.0000	0.0013	0.0173
	1.5	0.929	0.411	5.02	11.35	0.0571	0.1465	0.0765	0.0206	0.1179	0.1377	0.0748	0.2492	0.0227	0.2376	0.0018	0.0956	0.0000	0.0000	0.0010	0.0182
	2.0	1.013	0.399	5.23	13.29	0.0527	0.1586	0.0756	0.0234	0.1120	0.1547	0.0660	0.2750	0.0173	0.2514	0.0012	0.0969	0.0000	0.0000	0.0007	0.0188
0.75	0.4	0.679	0.431	4.42	6.97	0.0717	0.1059	0.0791	0.0133	0.1344	0.0902	0.1029	0.1681	0.0449	0.1792	0.0054	0.0870	0.0000	0.0000	0.0063	0.0283
	0.6	0.761	0.407	4.61	8.62	0.0672	0.1157	0.0783	0.0155	0.1291	0.1031	0.0941	0.1873	0.0386	0.1918	0.0044	0.0889	0.0000	0.0000	0.0057	0.0298
	1.0	0.912	0.373	4.96	12.13	0.0600	0.1331	0.0768	0.0198	0.1195	0.1287	0.0797	0.2217	0.0294	0.2119	0.0029	0.0917	0.0000	0.0000	0.0045	0.0325
	1.5	1.080	0.343	5.34	16.82	0.0524	0.1538	0.0751	0.0251	0.1095	0.1582	0.0660	0.2580	0.0218	0.2304	0.0020	0.0940	0.0000	0.0000	0.0035	0.0350
	2.0	1.229	0.322	5.68	21.69	0.0481	0.1668	0.0737	0.0301	0.1004	0.1854	0.0554	0.2882	0.0167	0.2438	0.0014	0.0954	0.0000	0.0000	0.0028	0.0367
1.00	0.4	0.673	0.410	4.59	7.55	0.0698	0.1045	0.0784	0.0134	0.1304	0.0903	0.0993	0.1652	0.0440	0.1755	0.0055	0.0861	0.0000	0.0000	0.0127	0.0394
	0.6	0.755	0.379	4.86	9.68	0.0648	0.1135	0.0772	0.0161	0.1234	0.1036	0.0896	0.1828	0.0377	0.1865	0.0044	0.0879	0.0000	0.0000	0.0113	0.0419
	1.0	0.910	0.334	5.36	14.62	0.0568	0.1301	0.0750	0.0211	0.1114	0.1292	0.0742	0.2138	0.0287	0.2040	0.0031	0.0903	0.0000	0.0000	0.0092	0.0461
	1.5	1.091	0.294	5.93	21.99	0.0492	0.1480	0.0725	0.0274	0.0991	0.1591	0.0603	0.2460	0.0214	0.2202	0.0022	0.0923	0.0000	0.0000	0.0074	0.0501
	2.0	1.260	0.266	6.45	30.58	0.0439	0.1622	0.0704	0.0339	0.0891	0.1868	0.0500	0.2727	0.0163	0.2318	0.0016	0.0938	0.0000	0.0000	0.0062	0.0533
$a_A = 0$				$a_B = 0$						TABLE 26a					$r_A = 0$				$r_B = 0$		
0.0	0.0	0.500	0.500	4.00	4.00	0.0833	0.0833	0.0810	0.0090	0.1470	0.0630	0.1250	0.1250	0.0630	0.1470	0.0090	0.0810	0.0000	0.0000	0,0000	0.0000

Fig. 3.4. American Portland Cement Association variable deck depth tables

of positive moments away from midspan. For simplicity, the deck AB is unit width and shown as fixed-ended with parabolic haunching to a deck depth at midspan half that at the supports.

For the unhaunched uniform depth deck, voiding will become possible as the span and the deck depth increase. For this reason, a typical voiding for the deck between the solid slab sections at the supports has been assumed to provide 25% weight savings. In the manner described in the DTp guide,[2] no allowance is made for the reductions in section modulus arising from the

Fig. 3.5 (above). Slab deck with and without haunching: (a) deck; (b) self-weight moments (concrete weight c per unit volume); (c) surfacing moments (surfacing weight s per unit area (uniformly distributed)); (d) live load moments; (e) differential-settlement moments (differential settlement Δ between A and B); (f) differential temperature moments (free rotation θ at A and B); (g) stresses

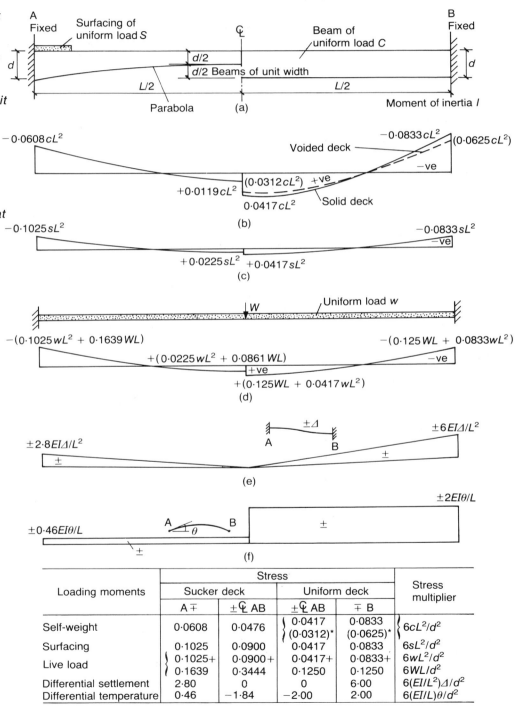

Loading moments	Stress				Stress multiplier
	Sucker deck		Uniform deck		
	A ∓	± ℄ AB	± ℄ AB	∓ B	
Self-weight	0·0608	0·0476	0·0417 (0·0312)*	0·0833 (0·0625)*	6cL²/d²
Surfacing	0·1025	0·0900	0·0417	0·0833	6sL²/d²
Live load	0·1025+ 0·1639	0·0900+ 0·3444	0·0417+ 0·1250	0·0833+ 0·1250	6wL²/d² 6WL/d²
Differential settlement	2·80	0	0	6·00	6(EI/L²)Δ/d²
Differential temperature	0·46	−1·84	−2·00	2·00	6(EI/L)θ/d²

*Voided deck.

(g)

voids, nor for that matter the moment-suction effects created by the stiffness differentials between midspan and support. The voided self-weight moment diagram is shown by a broken line in part (b) of Fig. 3.5, and the associated stresses in part (g) are shown within parentheses.

As the spans increase beyond 30 m, limited voiding is also possible on the sucker decks to further reduce weight. For spans exceeding 35–40 m, greater weight savings are possible by using hollow-box construction for both uniform depth and sucker decks. Fig. 3.5 does not cover these larger spans, but the advantages of localised depth savings obtained by the use of sucker decks still apply.

For the self-weight loading (Fig. 3.5(b)), the weight saving due to the haunching reduction is evident in the reduced moments at A and midspan AB and the reduced critical stress at A, even compared with the voided uniform depth slab (Fig. 3.5(g)).

For the uniform dead load of the surfacing (part (c) of the figure) and for typical applied live loads (uniformly distributed and single point loads) (part (d)), moments in the case of the sucker deck are reduced at midspan and correspondingly increased at the support. Stresses are increased at both midspan and support, the critical stresses again occurring at the support.

However, bending moments and stresses due to differential settlements (part (e)) and temperatures (part (f)), important in DTp's Combination 3 Loading, are much reduced for the sucker deck at midspan and supports.

As stated earlier, the self-weight reductions and the lesser effects of the differential settlement and temperature loadings are usually sufficient to offset the surfacing and live loading stress increases within the various required DTp loading combinations to maintain comparative depth d at the supports of the sucker deck. In the rare case that the depth d is insufficient, resort can be made to link-restrained compression steel. Alternatively, an increase in depth to $1.05d$ or $1.10d$ at the supports only should suffice, allowing for the increased moment suction which will be generated towards the support. This will still offer the localised depth savings at critical headroom locations within the span.

3.3. Bridge headrooms

Horizontal clearances and vertical headrooms required for bridges crossing UK roads and railways are standardised and given in DTp publications.[3,4] River and canal clearances, more often than not negotiated with the appropriate authority, can require differing headrooms over navigation channels, towpaths and so on. Individual obstacles, such as buildings, again generally require negotiation as to the amount of airspace to be left.

Fig. 3.6. Clearance problems

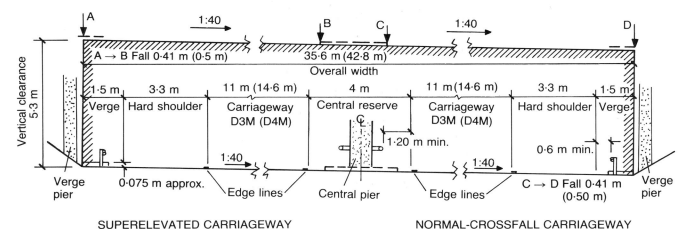

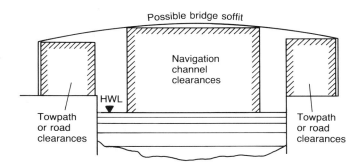

Fig. 3.7 (above). Clearances for dual three-lane and dual four-lane motorways: where dimensions differ, those for dual four-lane motorway are shown in parentheses

Fig. 3.8 (right). Typical river and canal clearances

As a slight diversion, Fig. 3.6 shows a European motorway bridge where both horizontal and vertical clearances in the fast lanes have only been maintained by a dangerous local protrusion of the central-reserve barrier on the unlit motorway. Not recommended!

Figures 3.7 and 3.8 show some clearance and headroom diagrams, specifically for UK motorways and generally for navigable-water crossings. It will be noted that the diagrams indicate varying absolute heights across the obstacles to be spanned. This is the feature which can be exploited by matching the minimum depth of the sucker deck to the underlying critical headroom of maximum absolute height. Motorway overbridge critical headrooms vary in absolute height because the underlying carriageways have significant crossfalls. As indicated in Fig. 3.7, these crossfalls for a dual three-lane motorway (D3M) are about 0·41–0·485 m from outer verge to the central reservation, falling on a curved superelevated carriageway and rising on a normal-crossfall straight carriageway. The larger fall arises where the central reservation is raised and kerbed but the verge is not. The level changes increase to 0·50–0·575 m for a D4M.

Sections 3.4–3.7 show typical depth savings gained by using sucker decks for crossing motorways with normal-crossfall or superelevated carriageways, for carrying inclined side roads and for crossing highway interchanges.

3.4. Sucker decks over normal-crossfall carriageways

Figure 3.7 shows a minimum drop of 0·41 m in headroom from the highpoints over the central-reservation hard strips to the outer verge edges of a normal-crossfall dual three-lane motorway. This can be exploited to give sucker deck depth savings for horizontal-profile side roads using a clear span crossing of the motorway.

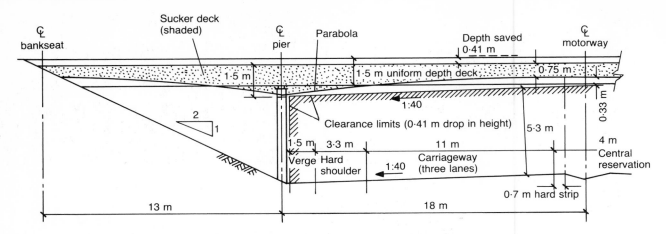

Fig. 3.9. Depth saving with three-span sucker deck over D3M

A typical three-span, uniform depth, voided deck horizontal crossing of a D3M would require 1·5 m depth to cater for continuous spans of 14 m, 36 m and 14 m, assuming cutting or embankment slopes of 1 : 2. An equivalent sucker deck would retain the 1·5 m depth at the pier supports but could reduce depths parabolically to as little as 0·75 m at deck centre and ends, depending on the degree of live loading.

Figure 3.9 shows that the uniform depth deck level is dictated by the headroom highpoints over the central hard strips, resulting in 0·41 m extra headroom over the verge edges. In contrast, the sucker deck level is governed by this verge headroom and the deck level can be dropped by 0·41 m, leaving excess headroom of 0·34 m over the hard strips. This allows the central depth of the sucker deck to be increased up to 1·09 m if required to cater for higher live loading without reducing the 0·41 m gain in level.

Thus the 0·5 m saving in level gained by adding continuity can be increased to at least 0·91 m by using the appropriate sucker deck. This can represent significant savings in earthworks and land acquisition in the case of approach embankments for elevated side road crossings and even more in the case of

Fig. 3.10 (right). M4 three-span sucker deck

Fig. 3.11 (below). M11 three-span sucker deck

Fig. 3.12 (above). M11 three-span sucker deck footbridge

Fig. 3.13 (right). M25 two-span sucker deck accommodation bridge

motorway cuttings for ground level side road crossings. Similar crossings of D4Ms and D2Ms would save 0·6 m and 0·4 m by the addition of continuity, increased to at least 1·1 m and 0·72 m respectively by the use of three-span sucker decks of similar shape.

Figures 3.10 and 3.11 show sucker deck road bridges which gained these sorts of earthworks savings for D3M cuttings. Fig. 3.12 shows a footbridge across a ground level D3M where the sucker design resulted not in earthworks savings but in a worthwhile 10% saving of the climbing height for the crossing pedestrian.

For D3Ms it is more customary to insert a pier in the central reservation. In the earlier example this would require four continuous spans of 14 m, 18 m, 18 m and 14 m, or two spans of 18·5 m and 18·5 m if abutments and wing walls were substituted for the outer spans. Both cases would require a uniform depth deck of some 1·0 m. A sucker deck can only be used to effect savings in deck level in this case when the side road profile is significantly convexly curved to allow aesthetically acceptable haunching over the central pier.

A typical symmetrical D3M two-span sucker deck, as shown in Fig. 3.2, uses two opposed parabolic soffits over the carriageway, cusping at a depth of 1·0 m over the motorway centre-line, reducing to 0·6 m over the abutments. The critical headroom in both spans is over the verge, the side road curved profile taking the deck soffit higher than the usually critical central headroom. In this instance the saving in level is entirely dependent on the sucker depth saving over the verge and not the available carriageway crossfall. It adds a minimum of 0·4 m to the 0·2–0·3 m gained by continuity. Fig. 3.13 shows a sucker accommodation bridge of this type effecting savings over a D3M. The lighter live loading has allowed the designer to extend the twin spans to bankseats at the tops of the cutting slopes.

A further interesting example of using side road curvature to insert a sucker deck is shown in Fig. 3.14. The proposed dual two-lane expressway ran through a prime residential area of a Middle East city and was depressed to minimise noise and visual intrusion. Unfortunately, groundwater rose as high as ground level itself and proved to be highly aggressive to both steel and

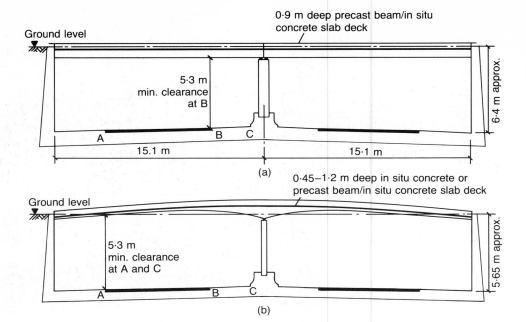

Fig. 3.14. Proposed depth saving with two-span sucker deck over Middle East depressed expressway: (a) uniform depth deck; (b) sucker deck

concrete. As a consequence, the expressway design required containment within a waterproofed reinforced concrete trough extensively ground-anchored to prevent flotation. The anchors needed a double skin protection against the surrounding 'chemical soup' and contributed to the very expensive trough construction, whose cost increased almost exponentially as the trough depth increased. Every effort was therefore made to minimise this depth.

The original intention was to carry the numerous ground level side roads horizontally across the expressway trough on two simply supported spans with a central pier. By adding curvature to the side road profiles, it was possible to substitute a continuous two-span sucker deck using opposed parabolically curved soffits.

As shown, while maintaining the critical headrooms, the sucker deck bridges allowed the expressway to be lifted by 0·75 m. This reduced the hydraulic pressures and flotation, with consequent savings in trough wall and floor thicknesses, besides numbers of ground anchors. In addition, the curved bridge decks not only drained better, they also looked more attractive.

3.5. Sucker decks over superelevated carriageways

Referring again to Fig. 3.7 it can be seen that the total drop in level between verges on a superelevated D3M is as much as 0·82 m. Sightline requirements for the curved motorway usually dictate the elimination of a central pier, resulting in the three-span type of deck shown in Fig. 3.15, with continuous spans of 14 m, 36 m and 16 m and a deck depth of 1·5 m. For a horizontal side

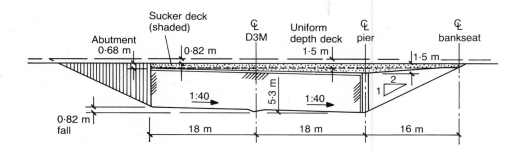

Fig. 3.15. Depth saving with three-span sucker deck over curved D3M

Fig. 3.16 (above). Super-elevated two-span sucker deck over M11

Fig. 3.17 (right). Super-elevated two-span sucker deck accommodation bridge over M11

road profile the critical headroom location is at the high-side verge, with an excess headroom of 0·82 m over the low-side verge.

In this situation the sucker bridge uses a straight-tapered soffit over the motorway, the deck depth varying from 1·5 m to 0·68 m. The appearance of the structure benefits from the insertion of an abutment and wing walls over the high-side cutting slopes and the provision of an opposing deck taper for the opposite side 16 m embankment span. The sucker deck can thus be lowered by 0·82 m. Compared with a series of three simply supported spans, the level change amounts to 0·5 m for continuity and 0·82 m for the sucker deck, a quite remarkable saving of 1·32 m.

The differences between 36 m and 16 m spans for this D3M bridge mean considerable uplift at the end of the short span, and most examples built possess other features which reduce the span differences. Fig. 3.16 shows a crossing where the embankment span nearly equals the 40 m D3M skew span because of the very flat embankment slopes required. In this case the inclined side road carried also assists in deck depth saving over the critical high point of the superelevated carriageway, as described in section 3.6. Fig. 3.17 shows even bigger equal spans on a two-span sucker deck crossing a superelevated D2M with separated carriageways. Both sucker decks used voiding to further reduce weight.

Similar sucker bridges over a fully superelevated D2M can save 0·64 m on the depth of a continuous uniform depth deck.

Fig. 3.18. Depth saving with four-span sucker deck over curved D3M

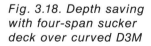

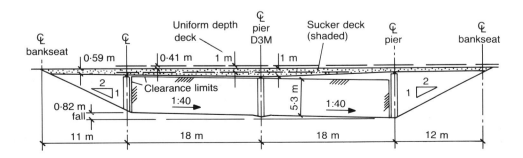

Fig. 3.19. Superelevated four-span sucker deck over M11

Occasionally, sightlines permit the inclusion of a central pier, leading to a four-span deck. Fig. 3.18 shows a deck with spans of 11 m, 18 m, 18 m and 12 m, and a depth of some 1·0 m over a fully superelevated D3M. The alternative sucker deck uses opposed straight-tapered deck spans over each carriageway, the taper matching the fall on the superelevated carriageway. The deck depths are 1·0 m at the centre and 0·59 m at the outer piers, continuing at that uniform depth over the embankment spans. The critical headroom location is again over the superelevated verge, allowing the sucker deck to be lowered by 0·41 m, with the usual savings. Fig. 3.19 shows a typical construction over a D3M. Figs 3.20 and 3.21 show an asymmetric twin-span sucker deck over a superelevated dual two-lane all-purpose road (D2APR) plus slip road.

3.6. Sucker decks carrying steeply inclined side roads

When the side road carried on bridge across the motorway is steeply inclined, it is possible to use a sucker deck to again effect significant earthworks savings, this time independent of the motorway crossfalls. The critical headroom location is at the outer edge of the verge underlying the low end of the bridge and, as always, the sucker deck soffit is arranged as a straight taper to give minimum deck depth over this location. The depth savings for such a deck as compared with a uniform depth deck can amount to 0·82 m for a D3M crossing.

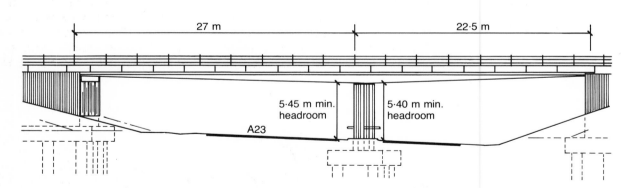

27 m   22·5 m

5·45 m min. headroom   5·40 m min. headroom

A23

Fig. 3.20 (above). Super-elevated two-span sucker deck over A23

Fig. 3.21 (right). Super-elevated two-span sucker deck over A23 bridge

Fig. 3.22. M11 two-span
steeply inclined sucker
deck

Such steep inclinations produce a noticeable asymmetry of elevation and no attempt should be made in the bridge design to overlay any symmetry. The bridge should add its own sympathetic asymmetry. The sucker deck taper assists in this, as do other asymmetric features on the example of a steeply inclined crossing of a D2M shown in Fig. 3.22.

Figure 3.23 shows a two-span sucker bridge carrying a steeply inclined and vertically curved urban side road. One span crosses the D3M in the foreground, and the second span crosses a series of rail tracks hidden in the background. In this case the deck depth increase over the pier has been gained by using the side road curvature, with only minor inclinations of the soffit. The resulting minimum deck depth is located over the farthest rail track, as evidenced by the smoke discoloration on the deck. A two-span uniform depth deck would have required the raising of the existing side road profile at least 1 m higher over the critical rail track, with severe repercussions on the housing seen near the bridge.

Sections 3.4–3.6 have illustrated the advantages to be gained by using sucker deck bridges mainly over motorways. They apply in differing degrees for crossings of other types of highway.

3.7. Sucker decks over highway interchanges

The bridge engineer is regularly required to provide a crossing over a highway interchange. The highway crossed may have associated slip roads climbing or falling away from it, also requiring spanning by the bridge, which may itself be carrying another slip road. These situations offer very good opportunities for making local depth savings by use of sucker decks, with significant economies in land acquisition and earthworks or bridge deck length.

Fig. 3.23. M1 two-span
curved and inclined
sucker deck

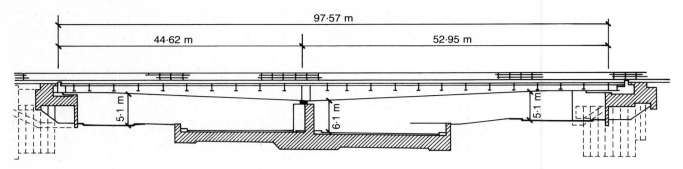

Fig. 3.24. Two-span railway sucker deck over German highway interchange

Figure 3.24 shows a European interchange crossed by a two-span railway bridge. The two slip roads are some 2·5 m higher than the motorway and are the critical headroom locations for the box girder bridge. The sucker deck soffit is fashioned as two opposed shallow curves with depths varying between 3·5 m at the central pier and 1·75 m at the ends. The depth saving for this design as compared with a uniform depth deck is considerable, at some 1·5 m.

A different layout is shown in Fig. 3.25, where the ground level slip roads are lower than the main highway, which is built on a low ramp. In this case the single-span crossing of the highway and slip roads is the centre of a long viaduct rising and falling back to ground level at the maximum permissible grade of 4% to minimise the overall length. The critical headroom for the curved profile main span is at the outer edge of the superelevated highway and the sympathetic sucker deck soffit is parabolic, with deck depth varying between 1·2 m at the piers to 0·8 m at midspan. The depth is less than that of a uniform depth deck by about 0·4 m, allowing a saving in viaduct length at each end of 0·4 divided by the 4% grade, a total length of 20 m.

3.8. Other advantages of sucker decks

In the span range 20–40 m, sucker decks are generally more effective in saving deck weight than the use of voids in equivalent uniform depth decks. This was demonstrated in the lesser self-weight bending moments and stresses shown in Fig. 3.5, which compared a solid concrete slab sucker deck with an equivalent voided slab uniform depth deck. Probably an even more important advantage lies in the elimination of the use of void formers, at least in this span range.

As with smoking, voided slab construction should carry a health warning. Over the years there have been a number of demolitions of newly constructed voided slab bridge decks due to concrete honeycombing and void movement during placing.

Fig. 3.25. Brent Cross Shopping Centre Viaduct, London

Fig. 3.26. Problems with deck voiding

Fig. 3.27 (below). M4 three-span sucker deck over River Loughor, Wales

Fig. 3.28. Derby Inner Ring Road bridge

The fact that concreting is always going to be difficult through the confined spaces between the void formers, particularly when ducted prestressing cables and/or congested reinforcement add further obstruction, seems to be a lesson which has to be learned the hard way by some contractors.

It was once thought that two-stage construction was the answer, even though differential early thermal shrinkage effects between the stages required extra slab reinforcement. This allowed easy pouring and inspection of the first-stage bottom flange, where honeycombing is liable to occur in single-stage construction. However, although integrity of the bottom flange could be readily assured, honeycombing of the second-stage webs and upper flange, together with void movement, was still possible. Indeed, any problems in the webs were out of sight and not easily detected.

Figure 3.26 illustrates a badly poured second stage of a voided prestressed concrete slab bridge deck. It was only chance which led to inspection by the cutting away of the large polystyrene void formers. Revealed was the obstructive effect of the web prestressing ducts. The concrete shown above the unplanned voids had stalled at descending any further, while the concrete below had proved more accommodating by fully descending on the other side of the duct obstruction and rising to almost cover up for its stickier partner.

Fig. 3.29. Two-span sucker deck footbridge over M1

Fig. 3.30 (below). Two-span sucker deck footbridge proposed for Severn Crossing, Shrewsbury: (a) elevation; (b) cross-section

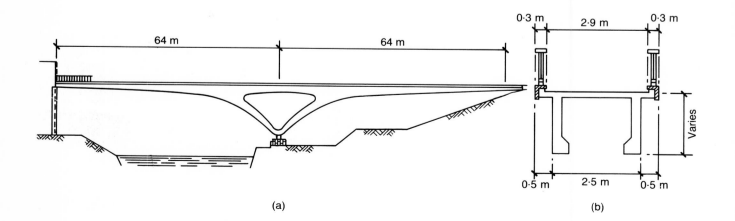

(a)

(b)

The use of an equivalent sucker deck would have eliminated this often problematical form of construction.

It is also evident that a well chosen sucker deck depth variation can enhance the appearance of a bridge. Most people like arches and curved soffit bridge decks (which tend to be labelled as arches). For many bridges, particularly over rivers, curved soffit sucker decks are used more for appearance than for the deck depth savings which arise in this design as compared with the alternative solution of a uniform depth deck. Examples are shown in Figs 3.27 and 3.28. Footbridges generally are expected to show more aesthetic adventurousness than road bridges and, again, a sucker deck shape can assist. Examples are shown in Figs 3.29 and 3.30.

3.9. References

1. AMERICAN PORTLAND CEMENT ASSOCIATION. *Handbook of frame constants.* APCA, Skokie, Illinois, Engineering Bulletin EB034D.
2. DEPARTMENT OF TRANSPORT. *User guide for slab and pseudo slab bridge decks.* HECB/B1/7.
3. DEPARTMENT OF TRANSPORT. *Cross-sections and headroom.* Departmental Standard TD 27/86.
4. DEPARTMENT OF TRANSPORT. *Railway construction and operation requirements, structural and electrical clearances.*

Pseudo sucker decks: *counterweights and cantilevers*

Fig. 4.1. Accommodation bridge over M11

4.1. What is a pseudo sucker deck?

The term 'pseudo sucker deck' evolved as a somewhat tongue-in-cheek expression to describe two further types of bridge deck which exhibit the typical depth variation of a sucker deck but either do not possess, or only partially possess, the stiffness differential 'moment-sucking' structural capacity described in chapter 3. Nevertheless, they do exhibit a capacity for reducing midspan sagging moments by other means, with the usual depth saving and aesthetic advantages.

One type, relatively a rare bird, is essentially a single simply supported span with short cantilever counterweight overhangs at each end. The other type, generally labelled as cantilever construction, is commonly used for large, longer-span viaducts where construction scaffolding is difficult or impossible to erect from ground level.

4.2. Counterweight decks

The attachment of short and heavy cantilever counterweights at the ends of a simply supported deck provides large hogging moments over the supports which reduce the midspan self-weight bending moments, sufficient to allow midspan deck depth reductions compared with a normal uniform depth simply supported span.

Early examples of this type of construction are described in a 1950s book on bridging,[1] whch mentions spans of up to 150 m. One bridge is shown in Fig. 4.2. It was built as an 18 m wide road bridge in California in 1941, and is remarkably slender for a reinforced concrete cellular slab spanning some 38 m. The self-weight sagging bending moment is greatly reduced by the hogging moments created by the gravel-container counterweights, permitting the deck depth variation in the simply supported span. The associated central weight reduction itself assists the counterweighting in reducing midspan moments.

Thus, the saving in midspan deck depth arises from the counterweighting and not from the moment-sucking effect of the stiffness variations which would occur with a similarly haunched span built continuous with adjacent spans. Most of the depth reduction advantages of continuous sucker deck construction apply to the statically determinate counterweight deck. As a result of this determinacy, an additional advantage arises in that there are no differential settlement bending effects. However, the deflections of the deck ends under live and thermal loading, together with the long term deflections due to creep and shrinkage, can be significant and it is usual to add short (3–4 m long) run-on or transition slabs to avoid any ridging which might arise in the road surface.

Figures 4.3 and 4.4 show a 55 m span prestressed concrete girder river bridge built as part of the Derby Inner Ring Road in the late 1960s.[2] The overhangs, in this case concrete, extend some 15 m at each end and are hidden by the piers and sidelong wing walls. In this case the counterweights were built as cantilevers to reduce central self-weight sagging moments before bearings were inserted under the deck ends to create a three-span continuous sucker deck for superimposed loading. This removed the requirement for run-on

Fig. 4.2. Santa Paula Bridge, California

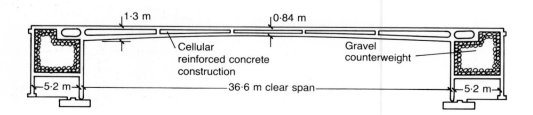

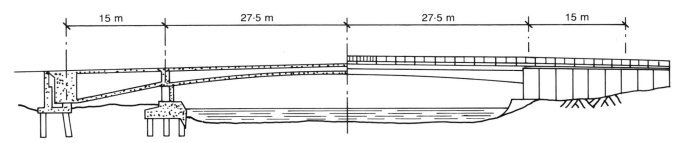

Fig. 4.3 (top). Causey Bridge, Derby Inner Ring Road

Fig. 4.4 (above). Causey Bridge counterweighting

slabs, but resulted in some long term redistribution of the self-weight moments due to creep and differential settlement.

Another type of counterweight deck is shown in Figs 4.1 and 4.5, one of several accommodation bridges built over the M11 in the 1970s. The simply supported span is some 38 m and the 15 m overhangs are set within the embankments without being supported by them. The resulting vertical deflections at the ends of the deck are catered for by the run-on slabs. In this case the attractively shaped deck is formed of voided reinforced concrete. The original design intention was to provide a hinged bearing at one support and a hinged sliding bearing at the other. However, to minimise maintenance requirements, hinged bearings were used at both supports. The structure is so slender that the portal action induced is only a minor extra effect compared with the dominant counterweighting action.

As with sucker decks, the midspan depth reductions allowed lowering of approach works, increased headroom or improved appearance.

4.3. Cantilever deck construction

In the case of cantilever construction, the deck is constructed as a sequence of free balanced cantilevers from each support pier before structural 'stitching' at each midspan location. At this stage, the now continuous multi-span

Fig. 4.5. M11 accommodation bridge counterweighting

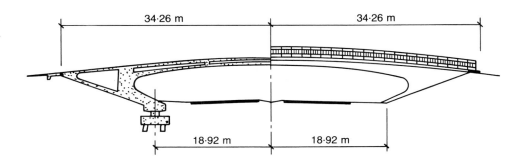

variable depth deck becomes a sucker deck for carrying all remaining super-imposed dead and live load.

As stated earlier, this type of concrete construction is chosen where ground-supported scaffolding cannot be used over water, traffic or other obstacles. Temporary support during erection is transferred to deck level by use of cantilever construction. Spans are generally greater than 50 m and the construction is normally of prestressed concrete staged segmental hollow box girders, either in situ or precast.

Fig. 4.6. Cantilever con-struction of A5 and A406 flyovers, Staples Corner Interchange, London

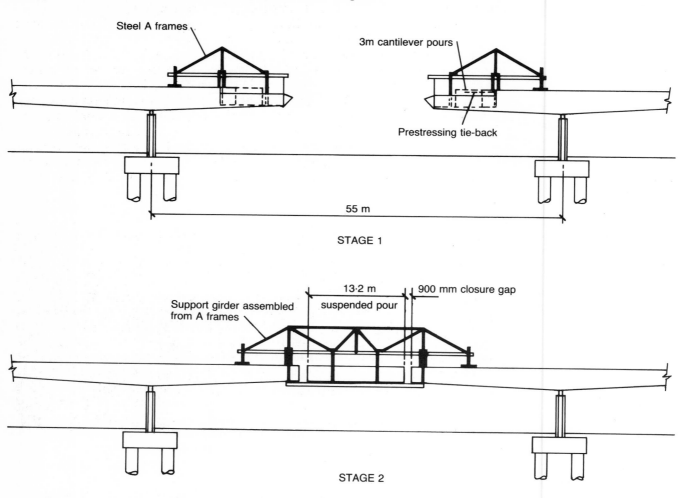

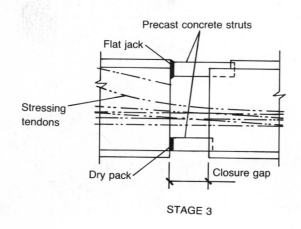

1. Place struts, free at one end.
2. Dry pack free end lower struts early morning.
3. Partially stress lowest cable in each rib.
4. Insert flat jacks free end top struts. Test and lock off at 0·1 MN.
5. Cast closure concrete to complete box girder.
6. Remove jacks after 24 hours and fill jack pockets with concrete.
7. Fully stress all tendons after 2½ days.
8. Remove falsework.

Figure 4.6 shows the cantilever construction method used for the in situ decks of two large flyovers built over a heavily trafficked road intersection in North London during the 1970s. The 55 m spans are formed of tapered cantilevered sections 20 m long, with a straight suspended section 15 m long. The cantilevers are constructed in 3 m long sections cast symmetrically outwards from each pier using temporary framed steel supports for each new pour, tied back to the previous pours, which have been cast and prestressed in a staged sequence. A temporary prop is erected near the pier support to cater for any out-of-balance loading during construction.

On completion of the cantilevering, the short uniform depth midspan section is cast on truss formwork supported by the ends of the cantilever sections. With considerable individual rotations occurring at the ends of the cantilevers and suspended central section due to temperature and differential temperature bending, small gaps are left before the ends of the independent cantilevers and suspended span are finally joined. This is undertaken by use of temporary steelwork or jacking to effect monolithic differential rotation-free connections while the joint concrete is poured and later prestressed.

Self-weight bending in the structure is thus taken mainly as statically determinate cantilever bending in the cantilever support sections and simply supported bending in the uniform depth central section. With the joints

Fig. 4.7. Cantilever construction of A406 flyover: note the props

Fig. 4.8. Construction of A406 flyover: closure span between cantilevers

Fig. 4.9. Cantilever construction of River Torridge bridge (design and supervision by MRM Partnership)

Fig. 4.10. Cantilever construction of bridge over Columbia River, Oregon

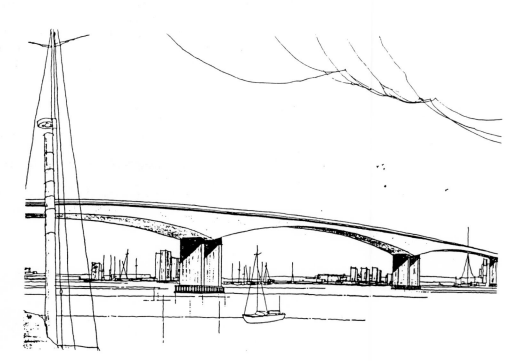

Fig. 4.11. Early alternative design for East London Crossing of River Thames

Fig. 4.12. Finback bridge, Austin, Texas (design and supervision by Tony Gee + Quandel)

between the two sections completed, the structure becomes a continuous sucker deck for further superimposed dead and live loading plus differential temperature, shrinkage and settlement effects.

The sucker action is thus only a partial one, and the sucker shape itself arises more from the tapered deck depth which best suits cantilever construction, rather than from any deliberate choice of a sucker shape of deck. Nevertheless, the usual midspan deck depth savings apply. They were used in these flyovers over critical headroom locations on the underlying roads to lower the flyover road profile, with significant savings in approach ramps. Figs 4.7 and 4.8 show different stages during the construction of these flyovers.

Even larger cantilever decks are constructed over water crossings and Figs 4.9[3] and 4.10 show recent examples, including the now commonly preferred epoxy-jointed, rather than concrete-jointed, segmental construction. The use of twin-walled piers, shown in Fig. 4.11, can offer construction advantages by providing out-of-balance support during cantilevering, requiring less temporary propping. Appearance is also improved because the deck soffit cusps are clearly visible and not obscured by a single wall pier located directly below.

A recent new form of cantilever construction has haunched inverted Ts built above road level within the central reservation (Fig. 4.12). These bridges, described as finbacks or sail types,[4] offer low construction depths below road level and could prove useful where headroom is tight.

4.4. References

1. LEGAT *et al. Design and construction of reinforced concrete bridges.* Concrete Publications Ltd, London, 1948.
2. DAVIES and RICHARDSON. St Alkmunds Way, Derby. *Highw. Engr*, 1973, Nov.
3. POTHECARY *et al.* Torridge Bridge: design and construction. *Proc. Instn Civ. Engrs*, Part 1, 1990, Feb.
4. GEE. Concrete finback bridge in USA. *Proc. Instn Civ. Engrs*, Part 1, 1991, Feb.

5

Precast concrete beam continuity:
benefits of continuity plus factory qualities

Fig. 5.1. M11 South Woodford Interchange viaducts

5.1. Precast prestressed concrete beam decks

Precast concrete beam bridge deck construction has been in use for a long time and its advantages of ease and speed of erection, elimination of obstructive falsework, standardisation and factory qualities brought to site are well known. As a result, it is one of the most favoured deck construction techniques for bridge decks of small to medium span.

The most commonly used prestressed beams are the M and U series, supporting and composite with an in situ reinforced concrete deck slab. Multi-span bridges rarely feature continuous decks (Fig. 5.1), and are usually built as a sequence of simply supported spans. With bearings required under each beam, support piers are of deck width, formed as either solid leaf or columns and crosshead arrangements (Fig. 5.2).

Beams in the M series were originally intended for contiguous assembly at 1 m centres to approximate to the structurally efficient voided slab construction. However, the need for inspection access between beams has led to the adoption of deeper beams spaced at up to 1·5 m.

The precast concrete manufacturers have recently introduced the Y beam[1] (Fig. 5.3), which better suits the needs of spaced beam and slab construction.

5.2. Deck continuity

As stated in section 5.1, precast concrete beam deck construction has generally been limited to simply supported structures. When the deck is multi-span, it is easier to design and construct it as a sequence of simply supported spans than to incur the added complexity and time penalties by adding continuity. These difficulties are often more perceived than real. As a result, the multi-span simply supported decks suffer the usual extra first costs due to the depth of construction and increased substructure sizes, together with extra maintenance costs due to the deck joints, all as referred to in chapter 2.

In addition, multi-span simply supported decks are usually confined to straight or near-straight alignments because of difficulties in fitting straight beam elements into curved decks. Plan curvature requires varying beam

Fig. 5.2. Typical simply supported precast concrete beam decks

lengths across the width of each span, removing most of the benefits of standardisation. Tight vertical curvature leads to excessive in situ deck slab build-up at midspan of the chorded beams, adding unnecessary deck depth and weight.

As a result, this form of construction has rarely been considered for flyovers convoluted both in plan and vertical profile which are often found in tightly confined urban situations. The choice for concrete construction then generally goes to voided in situ slabs or to precast or in situ segmental box girder decks, all more naturally suited to the problems of continuity and curvature.

However, the emphasis is changing and continuity is now a highly desirable feature because of the reduction of expansion joints. Corrosion caused by winter de-icing salts is currently the most damaging threat to the integrity of UK bridges. Recent investigations for the Department of Transport (DTp)[2] have confirmed that most bridge deck expansion joints leak and contribute more than any other bridge element to deck and substructure corrosion damage. The joints themselves also have a poor maintenance record.

Precast concrete decks invariably carry, and act compositely with, an in situ concrete deck slab. Why not use some of the in situ concrete construction in the pier area, where it is well suited to solving the problems of curvature and

Fig. 5.3. Precast concrete Y beam

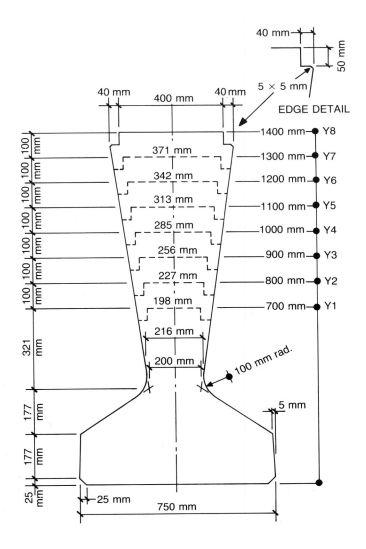

continuity, besides offering further advantages in pier construction and deck drainage arrangements? Confining this construction to an area over the pier foundations, which give readily available support for staging, with end-embedded precast beam/in situ slab construction in the deck areas between, provides the individual advantages of in situ and precast construction where they are best suited.

The DTp is currently preparing an advice note which will encourage the use of continuity in multi-span bridge decks in order to achieve the desirable reduction of expansion joints. With the precast concrete beam deck representing one of the most commonly used forms of deck construction, the DTp and the Transport and Road Research Laboratory (TRRL) recently commissioned a study of the ways in which continuity can be provided for composite bridge decks where the primary beams are of pre-tensioned precast concrete.[3] The study was followed by a survey[4] of 20 bridges featuring the various continuity connections, some of which were more than 20 years old. All connections were found to be in good to excellent condition, underlined by the fact that nearly half of the same bridges showed significant deterioration at leaking end joints.

The DTp–TRRL study identified five distinct methods of building-in various degrees of continuity and eliminating deck expansion joints in the UK. Some of the methods are also used internationally. One of the methods also overcomes most of the problems of urban flyover curvature described earlier.

The classification of the methods indicated that two make only the deck slab continuous or hinged over the piers, while the other three provide full monolithic continuity connection of the beams and slab over the piers.

All methods require in situ concrete transverse beams at or near the piers. These beams can be arranged as twin, one either side of the pier, or singly, located over the pier. Transverse beam depth can be less than, equal to, or greater than the longitudinal beam depth. For clarity, single transverse beams located over the pier and pier bearings are designated as integral crossheads. All other transverse beams are designated as diaphragms.

The five types of continuity detail are described in sections 5.3–5.7.

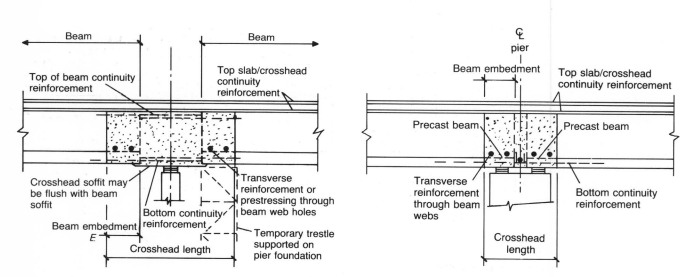

Fig. 5.4. Type 1 continuity connection: wide in situ integral crosshead

Fig. 5.5. Type 2 continuity connection: narrow in situ integral crosshead

5.3. Continuity detail type 1: wide in situ integral crosshead

The first type of continuity detail (Fig. 5.4) uses precast pre-tensioned beams significantly shorter than the spans between support piers and is the most commonly used UK method.

The beams, generally U or M type, are usually supported on temporary trestles built off the pier foundations. The wide in situ integral crosshead over the pier is then cast between and around the beams to provide about 1 m embedment. Longitudinal continuity is accomplished by reinforcement within the continuous composite deck slab, generally supplemented by reinforcement and, sometimes, pre-tensioning strand ends extending from the top and bottom of the embedded beams. Transverse strength is assured by either prestressing tendons or reinforcement, some of which may pass through holes in the ends of the precast beams.

The crosshead is supported on a single row of bearings set centrally on the pier.

5.4. Continuity detail type 2: narrow in situ integral crosshead

Figure 5.5 shows the second type of continuity detail, which is used extensively in America.

The precast pre-tensioned beams are long enough to be erected on two parallel rows of temporary or permanent bearings on the pier tops. As with type 1, the in situ integral crosshead over the pier is then cast between and around the beams to provide about 1 m embedment. The crosshead is, however, narrower than type 1 because of the necessarily small gap between the embedded beams. The same narrow gap makes adequate reinforcement connection difficult between beam ends. Longitudinal hogging bending continuity is again readily established by top reinforcement within, and extending well into, the continuous composite deck slab.

Transverse strength of the crosshead is generally provided for by reinforcement, some of which passes through holes in the ends of the precast beams.

Where twin rows of temporary bearings are used, a central row of permanent bearings located under the crosshead is brought into use by removal of the temporary bearings after the crosshead concrete has gained sufficient strength. Some examples use a wide single permanent rubber bearing which acts as a seating for both beams.

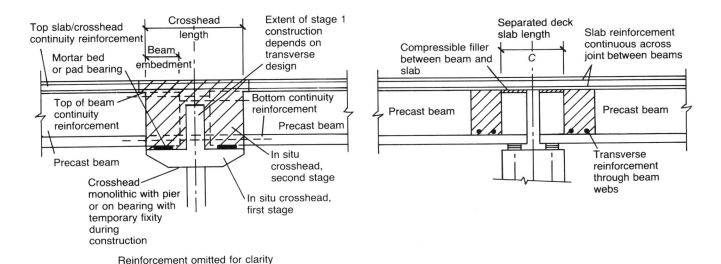

Fig. 5.6. Type 3 continuity connection: integral crosshead cast in two stages

Fig. 5.7. Type 4 continuity connection: continuous separated deck slab

5.5. Continuity detail type 3: integral crosshead cast in two stages

The third type of continuity detail (Fig. 5.6) is a variant of type 1 or type 2 where the integral crosshead is cast in two stages. The crosshead is of greater depth than the main deck precast beams and the bottom section is cast first to support these beams on thin mortar beddings. The second stage completes the integral crosshead in the manner described for type 2.

5.6. Continuity detail type 4: continuous separated deck slab

The fourth continuity detail (Fig. 5.7) confines itself to the deck slab only, which flexes to accommodate the rotations of the simply supported deck beams erected in the conventional multi-span manner. To permit this flexure, the deck slab is separated from the support beams for a length of about 1·5 m by a layer of compressible material. In situ reinforced concrete diaphragms are located at the ends of the separated slab. The method is apparently the subject of a patent taken out by Dr A. Kumar of Kumar Associates, UK.

A variation of this method omits the diaphragms and is known as the continuity plate construction method.[5] This was introduced in America in the 1950s and tested and developed in Switzerland and Germany in the 1960s. In Bavaria, Germany, over 300 multi-span precast concrete beam bridges had been built by 1981 using this type 4 variant continuity detail. The construction has been reported as being practical, economical and durable and is still in use in Germany.

5.7. Continuity detail type 5: tied deck slab

Figure 5.8 shows the tied deck slab detail, which was developed for multi-span precast beam decks during the UK Standard Bridge exercise of the 1970s.[6] The bridge decks are designed and constructed in the conventional multi-span simply supported manner with slab trimmer diaphragms at the beam ends. These ends are, as with type 4, carried on two parallel rows of bearings on the piers.

Long connecting reinforcement dowels are incorporated at the slab mid-depth to tie the slabs together over the pier, eliminating expansion movement at deck level and permitting the use of a buried deck rotation joint. To permit this rotation, the dowels are debonded and sleeved from the surrounding slab concrete over short lengths either side of the joint. Also, the slab and trimmer beam downstands are 'necked' using compressible joint filler below and above the dowel connection.

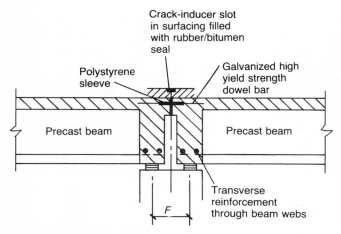

Fig. 5.8. Type 5 continuity connection: tied deck slab

Fig. 5.9. Type 5 joint after 15 years' use

Fig. 5.10. Support moments due to restrained deck creep and shrinkage: (a) structure; (b) creep; (c) shrinkage

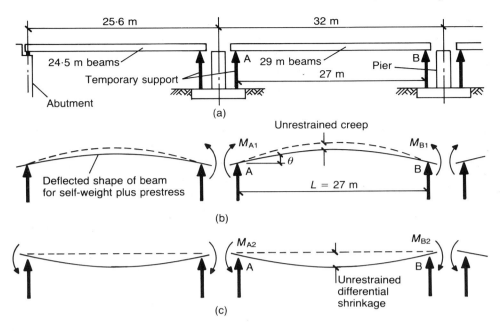

5.8. Choice of continuity method

If the main requirement is to eliminate troublesome intermediate deck expansion joints in multi-span decks, then types 4 and 5 offer the minimum of extra design and construction effort. The simplest procedure, type 5, however, is probably the least suitable because the tied deck joint retains a rotational capacity, with a sealed notch required in the deck surfacing. Nevertheless, the durability survey[4] showed type 5 deck joints up to 15 years old exhibiting no significant cracking, leakage or surface damage (Fig. 5.9).

However, to gain most of the advantages of continuity described in previous chapters, the method adopted should be type 1, 2 or 3. The deck bending reductions are more modest but still worthwhile in terms of construction depth savings, flyover lengths and associated ramps or earthworks. This is because the precast beam self-weight element remains simply supported and further continuity moments due to restrained creep and shrinkage of the beams must be considered in addition to the normal surfacing, live load and temperature loadings.

The embedment of the precast pre-tensioned beams into the in situ crossheads involves restraint to the continued prestressing creep rotation of the beam ends, giving rise to sagging moments at the supports. The beam ends rotate in the opposing direction due to the later differential shrinkage set up when the in situ concrete deck slabs are poured, giving rise to hogging moments over the supports. In general, the two moments tend to eventually cancel each other (Fig. 5.10). However, there is usually a delay of one or two months between beam embedment and slab pouring and the moments due to the restrained creep during that delay period must be considered alone for one of the design loading combinations.

In the following sections, the relative advantages of types 1 and 2 methods are listed. Type 3 method, representing an amalgam of types 1 and 2, is not particularly favoured for two reasons. Firstly, the downstand half of the crosshead is obstructive, both aesthetically and in terms of headroom. Secondly, to take advantage of a single row of bearings under the crosshead, special care must be taken during beam erection to prevent crosshead rotation and collapse. Fig. 5.11 shows such a collapse in the case of a bridge in Kuwait, which occurred because of unsymmetrical erection of the precast beams on each side of the crosshead.

Fig. 5.11. Collapse of type 3 connection due to asymmetrical beam erection

5.9. Relative merits of type 1 method

Type 1, the most commonly used method in the UK, is more complex to design and construct than any of the four other methods. Nevertheless, it offers more advantages, including the ability to accommodate plan and vertical curvature.

The key element is the wide in situ concrete integral crosshead, with temporary beam-support trestling and crosshead formwork supported off the pier foundations. The wide crosshead offers the following advantages.

(*a*) Precast beam deck spans are most often limited to the readily transportable length of 27·5 m defined by DTp. With 5 m wide crossheads and 1 m beam embedments, the continuous span lengths can be extended to 30·5 m. The usual end projecting reinforcement can be removed from embedded screw couplers to facilitate transport (Fig. 5.12).

(*b*) Plan curvature can be readily accommodated by variation of the width of the integral crosshead to form a trapezium shape in plan (Fig. 5.13). This overcomes the usual problem of the beams on the outside of the curve being longer than those on the inside and permits the use of one standard-length beam. The side curvature is taken up by variation of the width of the facing concrete (Fig. 5.14).

(*c*) Vertical curvature problems can be reduced by vertically curving the top and bottom surfaces of the crosshead. This reduces the increased slab thickness at midspan required to take up the vertical curvature above the straight chorded precast beams.

(*d*) Drainage of surface water on multi-span viaducts ideally requires collector downpipes spaced no further apart than the pier support positions. This means lateral connecting piping between kerb gulley drains at the deck edges and downpipes within or attached to the sides of the piers. Normal simply supported composite beam span decks are so congested with precast beam ends over the piers that it is usually too difficult to pass the drainage pipes through. Resort has therefore to be made to ugly external piping passing very prominently down the deck sides, or to more complex longitudinal deck drainage systems (Fig. 5.15). The type 1 continuity method uses wide in situ integral crossheads with the precast beam ends embedded some distance from the pier. This readily allows enough room for the passage of a concealed internal lateral connecting drain using generous diameters and bends (Fig. 5.16).

Fig. 5.12 (above left). End reinforcement projecting from beam in type 1 connection

Fig. 5.13 (above right). Overcoming plan curvature

Fig. 5.14 (below). Fascia curvature

Fig. 5.15 (right). External piping for deck drainage

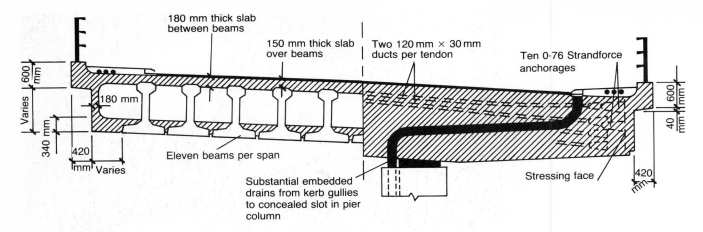

180 mm thick slab between beams

150 mm thick slab over beams

Two 120 mm × 30 mm ducts per tendon

Ten 0·76 Strandforce anchorages

600 mm

Varies

180 mm

340 mm

420 mm Varies

Eleven beams per span

Substantial embedded drains from kerb gullies to concealed slot in pier column

Stressing face

600 mm

40 mm

420 mm

Fig. 5.16. Concealed drainage piping

(e) Type 1 uses a single central row of bearings. This immediately halves the number of bearings required for simply supported construction, although individual bearing size will marginally increase.

(f) Piers are thinner, not only because a single line of central bearings takes up less room at the pier top, but because the dead and live load moments applied to the piers by off-centre pairs of bearings are removed. Significant savings in pier foundations also result.

(g) Full-width piers or crossheads are not required either. The integral crosshead in the deck can be top reinforced or prestressed laterally to allow considerable deck cantilevering outside the pier (Fig. 5.17). Resulting inboard piers can offer considerable savings in ground intrusion. This in turn can allow ground level slip roads to be located under

Fig. 5.17 (left). Inboard piers

Fig. 5.18 (below). Viaduct construction, M11 South Woodford Interchange

*Fig. 5.19. Transverse
crosshead prestressing*

the deck edges and can reduce flyover spans at skew crossings, both particularly important in cramped urban locations (see chapter 7). There is also a useful saving in further numbers of bearings.

The largest use of the type 1 method in the UK was during the construction of the six-viaduct London–Cambridge M11 South Woodford Interchange in 1976[7] (Figs 5.1 and 5.18). This was followed by the construction of two further similar viaducts forming part of the South Woodford to Barking Relief Road in 1987. The earlier construction benefited from a large degree of standardisation, with only two types of site-cast M beams required: 429 M8 beams 29 m long were used for the interior 32 m spans and 110 M8 beams 24·5 m long for the end 25·6 m spans.

The integral crossheads were transversely prestressed (Fig. 5.19), as much as anything to avoid congestion in the upper surface due to heavy transverse and longitudinal reinforcement. Tests of the crosshead were undertaken at the then Cement and Concrete Association at Wexham Springs[8] (Fig. 5.20). These demonstrated the effectiveness of the shear transfer between the beams and crosshead and proved the method to be entirely successful. Nevertheless, the

*Fig. 5.20. Testing a type 1
connection*

transverse prestressing is expensive and later constructions have resorted to the use of normal steel reinforcement rather than prestressing.

5.10. Relative merits of type 2 method

Type 2 is almost the only continuity method used in America and is easier to build than type 1. Nevertheless, it cannot offer the advantages of extra span, curvature or drainage offered by type 1. In most cases, it also does not offer the bearing and pier advantages, unless beams are seated on temporary twin rows of bearings and loads are eventually transferred to a permanent single row of bearings set under the integral crosshead, or use is made of a wide single bearing.

Undoubtedly, the greatest advantage of the type 2 method lies in the ease of placing the precast beams directly on to the piers. Nevertheless, the narrower integral crosshead makes adequate reinforcement connection difficult between beam ends (Fig. 5.5), particularly for sagging moment bottom reinforcement.

A recent American report has proposed that the provision of this bottom reinforcement should be optional provided that continuity moments are calculated assuming lack of positive-moment continuity.[9] It is also suggested that any cracking resulting from this reinforcement not being provided is no threat to the deck integrity and will certainly eliminate any corrosion possibility. No doubt a compromise solution could be used—a limited amount of anti-crack reinforcement in the bottom of the crosshead, possibly epoxy-coated to prevent corrosion.

Major research and testing of the type 2 connection was undertaken by the American Portland Cement Association in Chicago in the early 1960s.[10] It covered all aspects, ranging from creep and shrinkage to horizontal shear connection. It also covered extensive testing of a half-scale continuous two-span deck, some 20 m long by 5 m wide.

A recent UK publication[11] sets out design procedures for using type 2 continuity for the new precast Y beams.

5.11. References

1. TAYLOR *et al.* The Y-beam. *J. Instn Struct. Engrs*, 1990, Dec.
2. WALLBANK. *The performance of concrete in bridges: a survey of 200 highway bridges.* HMSO, London, 1989.
3. PRITCHARD and SMITH. *Investigation of methods of archieving continuity in composite concrete bridge decks.* Transport and Road Research Laboratory, Crowthorne, 1991, TRRL/DTp Contractor Report CR 247.
4. PRITCHARD and SMITH. *A survey of composite concrete bridge decks made continuous.* Transport and Road Research Laboratory, Crowthorne, 1991, TRRL/DTp Contractor Report CR 294.
5. WAGNER and BUCHTING. Continuity plate construction in multi-span bridges using precast concrete beams. *Bauingenieur,* 1981.
6. DEPARTMENT OF TRANSPORT. *DTp standard bridges.* HMSO, London, 1979.
7. PRITCHARD. Integral in situ crossheads for continuous precast beam deck viaducts. International conference on short and medium span bridges, Toronto, 1982.
8. STURROCK. *Tests on model bridge beams in precast to in situ concrete construction.* Cement and Concrete Association, Wexham Springs, 1974.
9. *Design of precast prestressed bridge girders made continuous.* USA Transportation Research Board, 1989. National Cooperative Highway Research Programme Report 322.
10. MATTOCK *et al.* Precast concrete bridges. *Journal of Research and Development Laboratories, Portland Cement Association, USA,* 1960–61.
11. HAMBLY and NICHOLSON. *Prestressed beam integral bridges.* Prestressed Concrete Association, Leicester, 1991.

6

Draped and hybrid prestressed precast concrete beams: *pre-tensioning and post-tensioning combined*

6.1. Special requirements for pre-tensioned precast beam continuity
6.2. Draped tendon pre-tensioned precast beams
6.3. Hybrid prestressed precast beams
6.4. References

Fig. 6.1. Hybrid beams, Kuwait

6.1. Special requirements for pre-tensioned precast beam continuity

For simply supported precast beam decks, the prestressing tendons are located at maximum eccentricity in the midspan regions, where the deck self-weight bending compressive stress in the top flange counters any tensile stresses due to the eccentric prestress. At the ends of the beam this self-weight compressive stress is lost and the prestress eccentricity must be reduced to give no tensile stress in the top flange.

In post-tensioned beams, the tendon profiles can be readily tailored to provide the reduced end eccentricity. In factory-made pre-tensioned beams, the eccentricity is usually reduced by debonding some of the tendons, using suitable end sheathing. An alternative sometimes used for longer beams is to mechanically deflect some of the tendons on the stressing bed prior to casting and subsequent tendon release. End-debonding of some of the remaining undeflected tendons is usually required in addition.

When the decks are continuous, as with types 1, 2 and 3 methods described in chapter 5, the requirements for the prestressing of the precast beams change. The embedded beam ends are now located in a hogging bending region and it is no longer sufficient to eliminate tensile stress in the top flange by reducing tendon eccentricity. The tendons must be lifted even further at the beam ends to produce compression in the top flange to resist tensile stresses due to hogging bending. This is particularly so with types 2 and 3 continuity methods as the embedded beam ends are closer to the maximum hogging bending over the pier.

To gain this extra eccentricity lift at the ends of precast pre-tensioned beams it is usual to adopt the mechanical deflection, or draped tendons, described earlier. Another possibility is a hybrid construction, combining undeflected pre-tensioning tendons with profiled post-tensioned tendons. Both these methods are described in sections 6.2 and 6.3.

6.2. Draped tendon pre-tensioned precast beams

The most common method of deflecting prestressing tendons is to pull them down from the long line pre-tensioning beds. A typical procedure is shown in Fig. 6.2. The high points of the tendon profile, located outside or between the beams in the production line, are supported by steel pillar assemblies incorporating needle roller-bearing supports for the tendons. The low points of the profile, located between the beam third and quarter points, are held down by

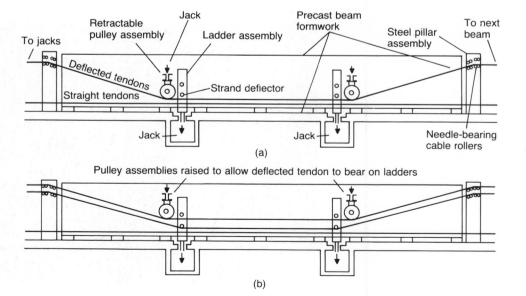

Fig. 6.2. Draped tendon pre-tensioning: (a) stage 1; (b) stage 2

steel ladder assemblies passing through the beam soffit into anchor pits built beneath the beds.

The stressing procedure is to thread pairs of strands with similar deflected profiles over the pillar supports and through the relevant slots in the ladders of each beam. A retractable pulley assembly is then lowered on to the two strands near the ladder positions at a level sufficient to hold the strands just clear of the ladder rung which will eventually hold down the strand pair. Individual jack stressing of the two strands then takes place at the bed anchor positions, the large pulley wheels and pillar rollers ensuring minimum friction. The pulley assembly is then retracted sufficiently to lay the stressed strands against the relevant ladder rung, thus transferring the tie-down load. Pulley retraction continues further to allow threading and stressing of the next pair of strands. The deflected strands are thus eventually anchored on to the ladder rungs.

After stressing it is necessary to cut off the steel ladder connections projecting through the beam soffits. To facilitate this operation, shallow pockets are left in these soffits, to be filled after the beams have been released from the stressing beds. There is sometimes concern that some of this non-prestressed filling material might, with the passage of time and loading, fall away—possibly to the danger of underlying traffic or pedestrians. Special pocket reinforcing techniques are needed. These are not always successful, as can be seen with the rusting of the 15-year-old pockets shown in Fig. 6.3.

Most of the 540 precast M beams required for the M11 South Woodford Interchange (shown in Figs 5.1 and 5.16) were pre-tensioned in this manner on a long line pre-tensioning bed set up on site (Fig. 6.4). For the 29 m beams, 14 of the 28 Dyform 15·24 mm dia. strands were deflected, while four of the remaining 14 straight strands were sleeve-debonded over the end 2 m.[1]

Another method of deflecting tendons is the 'mirror' technique (Fig. 6.5). An identical extra permanent strand system is provided above the long-line pre-tensioning beds and the beams under manufacture. The beam strands are deflected by being alternately clamped together with, and forced apart from, the overlying 'mirror' strand system, which is released back to its straight alignment after transfer for reuse. An advantage of this method is that the strand deflectors project out of the top of the beam and do not require exposed pockets and filling in the soffit.

Fig. 6.3. Rusting tie-down anchor pocket

Fig. 6.4. M11 Woodford
Interchange beam pre-
tensioning

6.3. Hybrid prestressed precast beams

The hybrid method of providing tailored varying tendon eccentricity in pre-tensioned precast beams was developed for a large number of bridge beams required for the Fahaheel Expressway in Kuwait in 1980.[2] Some 17 bridges required approximately 500 AASHTO PCI type 4 precast concrete I beams up to 28·45 m long (Fig. 6.1). Stressing bed capacity and concrete strength limitations, together with a lack of tendon deflection facilities in Kuwait at the time, meant that a hybrid beam had to be designed, incorporating both pre-tensioned straight strands and a single draped post-tensioned cable (Figs 6.6 and 6.7).

The AASHTO type 4 beam fortunately has a web which is wide enough for a 65 mm tendon duct, and suitable anchors can be accommodated in the end faces of the beam within the top flange without recourse to the usual end block thickenings.

Fig. 6.5. Mirror pre-
tensioning

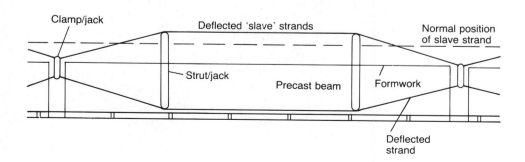

Fig. 6.6. Hybrid beam manufacture for the Fahaheel Expressway bridges, Kuwait

Fig. 6.7. Completed hybrid beams, Kuwait

Pre-tension strands were provided up to the available 400 t bulkhead capacity, and this allowed beams to be lifted off the pre-tensioning beds to the storage area as soon as the manageable transfer strength of 30 N/mm^2 was attained. Post-tensioning of the single cables to bring the beam up to its full strength, with 560 t prestress, could then be carried out away from the beds, when the 28 day concrete cube strength of 45 N/mm^2 had been achieved. As the available local concretes were stretched to gain this value, it can be seen that any attempt to provide full pre-tensioning over the long line bed would have required an uneconomic one month wait before transfer and beam bed release.

The draped post-tensioning cable also possessed the considerable advantages of enhancing the shear capacity of the beam and minimising the end tensile stresses, although some debonding of the pre-tensioned strands still proved necessary.

Obviously such hybrid beams could provide a highly efficient and possibly more economical substitution for the mechanically deflected tendons which have been used to date for precast beam continuity. A further advantage lies in the ability to lift the beams off the pre-tensioning beds at an early stage at lower transfer strengths.

Hybrid beams have been used to a limited extent abroad[3] since 1980 but the recent introduction of the Y beam in the UK now offers the chance to use the hybrid technique in the UK. The Y-beam web is wide enough to accommodate both post-tensioning ducts and end anchorages, the latter without recourse to end blocks.

6.4. References

1. PRITCHARD. The use of continuous precast beam decks for the M11 Woodford Interchange viaducts. *J. Instn Struct. Engrs*, 1976, Oct.
2. PRITCHARD and HEATHER. Kuwait 'hybrid' precast bridge beams. *Concrete Mag.*, 1981, July.
3. HARVEY. Hybrid precast concrete girder bridges. Second International Conference on Short and Medium Span Bridges, Ottawa, 1986.

NEW SUBSTRUCTURES

Inboard piers: *reducing landtake and simplifying skew*

7.1. Advantages of inboard piers
7.2. Reduction in landtake for urban interchanges
7.3. Skew bridge problems
7.4. Early 'squared-up' solutions to skew bridge problems
7.5. Squared-up skew bridges using inboard piers
7.6. Bridge standardisation
7.7. References

Fig. 7.1. A406 flyover construction, Staples Corner, London

7.1. Advantages of inboard piers

Inboard piers may be defined as deck supports which are narrower in plan than the bridge deck carried, with the deck edges cantilevering out beyond the pier edges (Fig. 7.1).

Inboard piers exploit the often ignored transverse and torsional strengths and stiffnesses available in a continuous multi-span deck, which is generally designed and proportioned according to bending and shear considerations in the longitudinal direction. A typical continuous slab deck has as much transverse cantilever bending and shear strength available at the pier locations as it has longitudinally, provided that the top transverse reinforcement or pre-stressing, plus the shear reinforcement, is designed accordingly. This can even permit full deck cantilevering of a torsionally stiff deck either side of a single central column pier (Fig. 7.2), which is about as far inboard as one can get!

The use of inboard piers can offer the designer several advantages

(a) reduction in landtake for urban interchanges
(b) minimising the problems of multi-span skew decks
(c) improved sightlines for vehicles passing the inboard piers
(d) better appearance.

The first two advantages listed can offer considerable economies, which are covered in the following sections.

7.2. Reduction in landtake for urban interchanges

Figure 7.3 shows alternative cross-sections of a multi-span urban interchange featuring a flyover and ground level slip roads. One deck is made up of a series of simply supported beam and slab spans, with full-width piers required to support the full-width spread of beams.

The second deck is formed from a continuous box girder with side cantilever slabs. In this case the pier is well inboard, its width being dictated by the room required to fix two deck support bearings. The bearing spacings are the minimum possible consistent with the need to provide the factors against bearing uplift due to eccentric deck loading required by clause 4.6.1 of BS 5400 part 2.

The extra ground space provided by the inboard piers can be utilised by tucking the ground level slip roads under the deck when the flyover has climbed sufficiently to provide the required headroom. This is not possible with the full-width piers of the flyover consisting of simply supported spans, where the slip roads can only be located outside the plan projection of the flyover deck.

Fig. 7.2. Multi-span single column support viaduct, Portsmouth

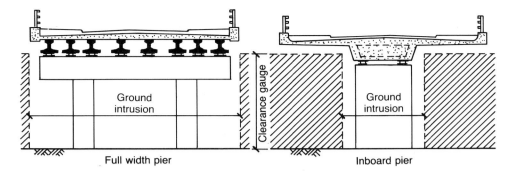

Fig. 7.3. Reduction in landtake under flyover

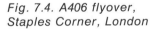

The savings in valuable urban land and any associated buildings can be considerable. For instance, a flyover carrying a dual three-lane urban road (Figs 7.1 and 7.4) can provide enough space underneath to accommodate two-lane ground level slip roads either side of the inboard piers (Fig. 7.5). This represents a landtake saving of some 15 m² per metre run of flyover. Allowing for end lengths where headroom is insufficient and roundabout lengths near the major road crossed by the flyover, this can mean a saving of about a hectare of urban land for a 600 m long flyover. With urban land valued at several hundred thousand pounds a hectare, it can be seen that the simple adoption of inboard piers offers considerable economy over conventional full-width piers.

Most urban interchanges provide hard landscaping under the flyover (Fig. 7.6), so further significant savings of about a hectare of hard landscaping also add to the landtake saving. More savings may result from the changes in flyover structural costs if the reductions arising from the smaller piers and foundations are greater than the cost of the extra transverse deck reinforcement at the piers.

Figures 5.14 and 7.7 show further examples of inboard piers on dual two-lane urban flyovers, where the possible savings are reduced, but still significant. In most of the urban flyover situations illustrated, full advantage

Fig. 7.4. A406 flyover, Staples Corner, London

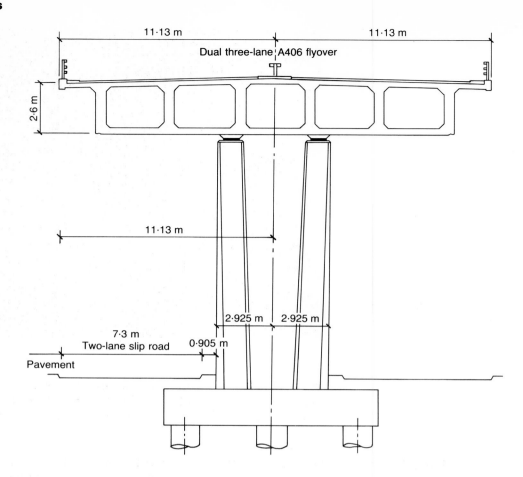

Fig. 7.5. Ground level slip roads under A406 flyover

Fig. 7.6. Hard landscaping under flyover, Liverpool

Fig. 7.7. Inboard piers, A5 flyover, Staples Corner, London

of the land and landscaping savings possible from the adoption of flyover inboard piers was not taken. This arose because landtake and slip road layout was planned in the early stages on the basis of full-width flyover piers.

7.3. Skew bridge problems

The ideal bridge crossing of any obstacle is a square crossing, which ensures minimum span, deck area and support pier lengths, with attendant economies. It is also the easiest structure to design and detail.

Unfortunately, road layouts, particularly those featuring interchange slip roads, often dictate crossings at angles other than square, requiring a skew

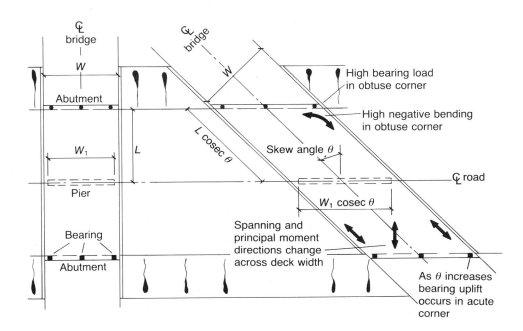

Fig. 7.8. Extra complexity and costs associated with skew

bridge. Further complications can arise if either or both of the bridge and the road, rail or river obstacles crossed are curved in plan, in which case the skew angle is defined by the intersecting centre-lines of bridge and obstacle.

Figure 7.8 shows typical two-span square and skew crossings of the same dual carriageway obstacle to demonstrate the extra costs and complexities of the skew alternative. Spans, deck areas and support lengths all increase in proportion to cosec θ, where θ is the angle of skew. Extra design complexities arise because the skew deck tends to span square between supports in the central deck areas and skew in the deck edge strips. As the skew angle increases, bearing reactions and associated negative bending moments increase in the obtuse angle corners, while bearing reactions change to uplift in the acute angle corners.

The highway engineer will occasionally present the bridge engineer with skew crossings in the 85° region, where the increases in span, area and support lengths approach twelvefold. The response from the latter might well be that if the former cared to add a couple more degrees of skew there would be no need for a crossing!

7.4. Early 'squared-up' solutions to skew bridge problems

In the 1950s and 1960s, UK bridge designers used deck design procedures based on longitudinally spanning foot-wide deck strips with distributed and concentrated live loading appropriate to these strips. The procedure was hardly appropriate to decks with any significant skew, although designs continued to be produced using the same foot-strip procedures, albeit spanning the greater skew span.

It is therefore not surprising that, when presented with a high-skew crossing, attempts were made to 'square up' the crossings in several ways to avoid at least the design complexities.

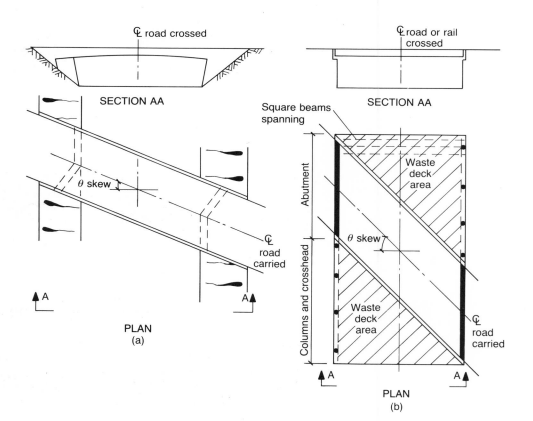

Fig. 7.9. Squaring-up arrangements:
(a) cutwater abutments;
(b) extension of supports and deck

Fig. 7.10. Cutwater-abutment bridge, M4, Gloucestershire

Figure 7.9 shows two typical squaring-up arrangements for highly skewed single span crossings. One uses a 'cutwater' face shape to the abutments, where one half of the face runs parallel to the road crossed and the other half is angled back to provide symmetry with the skew centre-line of the deck. In this case, the variable depth deck is formed from two anchored cantilever ends plus a drop-in central span (Fig. 7.10). The counterweighted pseudo sucker deck described in chapter 4 could equally have been used in this situation.

The other squaring-up arrangement is wasteful and visually very evident. The supports and deck are extended to make a square crossing at the considerable extra cost of the surplus untrafficked corners shown.

A further interesting example of dealing with skew is shown in Fig. 7.11. In this case the 85° skew required unsupported edge spans of 153 m. In the words of the designers:[1] 'By providing the principal stiffness along the shortest path

Fig. 7.11. Spine pier and cantilever deck proposal

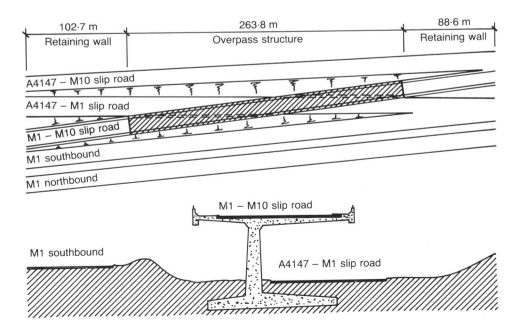

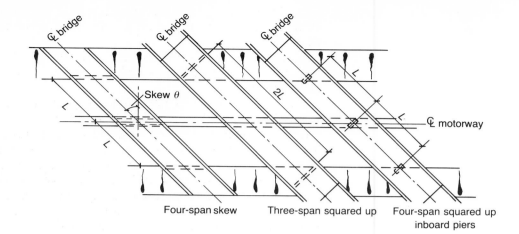

Fig. 7.12. Using inboard piers for skew decks

from the load to the support the extreme skew enables the deck to be cantilevered directly from the main walls.'

The problems of skew deck analysis began to clear in the late 1960s and the 1970s with the introduction of finite element computer programs and the publication of diagrams of principal moments in skew slabs.[2] Nevertheless, the technique of squaring-up has continued with narrow multi-span skew crossings by the more effective use of narrow inboard piers.

7.5. Squared-up skew bridges using inboard piers

Figure 7.12 shows three examples of continuous multi-span skew crossings of a motorway. The first is a typical complex four-span skew structure, with the skew created by full-width piers and bankseats running parallel to the motorway.

The second shows an attempt at squaring-up which suffers an over-long central span because a square full-width pier cannot be fitted into the narrow central reservation of the motorway.

The third shows how the use of narrow inboard piers allows a square pier to be located within the central reservation, with the resulting four square spans no greater than the four skew spans. The use of the available extra

Fig. 7.13. Churchill Way Flyovers, Liverpool

transverse bending and torsional strengths and stiffnesses of the deck in the third example are more than a trade-off for the skew problems of the first example.

The use of inboard piers for squared-up skew crossings occurred in Germany and California as early as the 1960s, with occasional use of central single bearing piers.[3]

An early example in the UK was the Tunnel Relief flyovers interchange (now known as Churchill Way) completed in 1970 at the entrance to the Mersey Tunnel, Liverpool.[4] Fig. 7.13 shows how the narrow two-lane pre-stressed concrete flyovers were supported on monolithic central circular columns which were narrow enough to fit into the reservations and verges of the heavily skewed ground level roads system crossed. This permitted a squared-up non-skew deck design for the ten-span continuous flyovers. Fig. 7.14 shows how the deck articulation and stability were handled, the circular columns being supported on corbels seated on twin roller bearings buried in inspection/maintenance pits located under the verges and reservations.

Improvements in bearings over the years and greater use of the generally unused but available torsional strength and stiffness of box girder decks allowed transfer of deck movements to the tops of the single central columns. For some time there was apprehension about extending single bearing supports to more than one or two spans, and Figs 7.15–7.18 show several examples of multi-span decks supported by twin bearing piers having single bearing supports inserted where ground space is lacking.

Recent structures, however, have produced squared-up multi-span skew bridges using central single bearing piers throughout. Fig. 7.19 shows a

Fig. 7.14. Articulation arrangements, Churchill Way Flyover

Fig. 7.15. Single column supports, M11 Woodbridge Flyovers, London

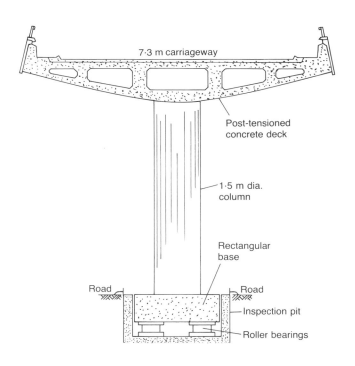

four-span 52° skew two-lane crossing of the M25 which was designed and built as a square bridge. The torsion is carried to each end bankseat support and resisted by outrigger support diaphragms (Fig. 7.20), which allow the end twin bearings to be spaced sufficiently to prevent bearing uplift in service. To provide the factors against this uplift required by BS 5400, tie rods capable of absorbing deck movements are located adjacent to the bearings.

The largest structure of this kind in the UK is shown in Figs 7.2 and 7.21. The multicell prestressed concrete box carries three lanes across seven 36 m spans supported only on narrow central columns via single bearings. Some on-site measurements to determine the vibration characteristics of this very long torsional deck showed satisfactory dynamic characteristics. The inves-

Fig. 7.16. Single bearing support, Fiveways Flyover, London

Fig. 7.17. Single column central reservation piers, M4/M25 Interchange, Heathrow, London

Fig. 7.18 (below). Single column central reservation pier, M11 bridge

tigation also demonstrated that the deck twist induced extra lateral bending in the support columns.

7.6. Bridge standardisation

The lessons of squaring-up were applied in an early proposal for the 1970s and 1980s UK Bridge Standardisation Project, where skew was the the dominant parameter.[5] The idea was that when several bridges of various geometries were required for a stretch of rural motorway or all-purpose road, the engineer would examine the 'bridge bank' files held by the Department of Transport and abstract several ready-detailed designs for each bridge—in simply supported or continuous spans, composite steel–concrete, reinforced or prestressed concrete, beam or slab, precast or in situ types of construction. An initial selection would discard some types, say because of headroom or soil problems, and the remainder would be put out to tender, together with bills and documents, also 'off the shelf'. The various tenderers would then price

Fig. 7.19 (right). Four-span single column pier bridge, M25

Fig. 7.20 (below left). Outrigger bankseat bearings on M25 bridge

Fig. 7.21 (below right). Multi-span single column pier viaduct, Portsmouth

only for the bridge types they thought economic. For skew bridges, each design and set of details could be used only for the precise skew angle involved. The proposal was to use squared-up designs where one basic bridge could cover a whole range of skews, vastly reducing the amount of design and stored detail.

Investigations indicated that central columns with single spherical bearings could be utilised for the narrow continuous reinforced concrete slab decks carrying one-lane or two-lane side roads over the main road without excessive twist due to off-centre live loading.

Fig. 7.22. Three-span standard bridge at 15° skew

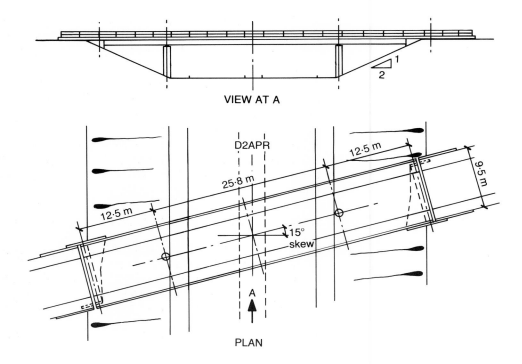

Fig. 7.23. Three-span standard bridge at 0° skew

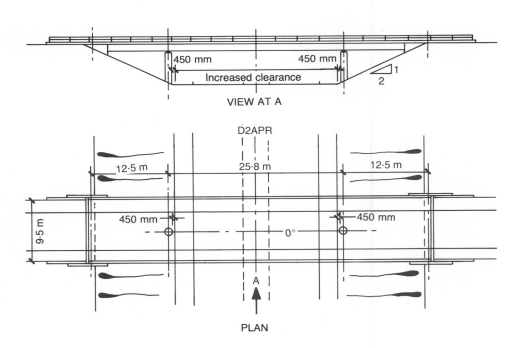

Cost exercises showed that a four-span overbridge at 25° skew, when squared up and using single-column supports, was marginally cheaper than the conventional skew-ended deck with tri-column piers placed parallel to the motorway. The deck construction depth remained similar, the 'peaking' of the longitudinal moments over the single central column being dealt with by local compression reinforcement.

The great advantage of this approach was that with slight overspanning one squared-up overbridge design could cover a large range of skews merely by rotation of the whole bridge arrangement in plan to the specific skew requirement.

Figure 7.22 shows a squared-up three-span overbridge with central single bearing column piers, designed to cross the underlying road at 15° skew. Any angle of skew below 15° can be accommodated by the simple rotation procedure.

Figure 7.23 shows the identical bridge arrangement used for a square crossing (i.e. 0° skew). The only penalty is the slight overspanning of 0·90 m arising from the rotation. Further one-design ranges of 25° to 15° were chosen to limit this overspanning.

Sadly, the proposed squaring-up was not adopted, a fate which eventually befell the whole UK Standard Bridge Project. Nevertheless, the concept remains a valuable aid to any bridge standardisation project.

7.7. References

1. GOODALL and PORTER. 85° angle overpass. *DoE Construction*, 1974, No. 12, Dec.
2. RUSCH and HERGENRODER. Influence surfaces for moments in skew slabs. Cement and Concrete Association, London, 1961, translation.
3. LEONHARDT and ANDRA. Problems of supporting elevated road bridges. Cement and Concrete Association, London, 1962, library translation 95.
4. BROWN *et al*. City of Liverpool Tunnel Relief Flyovers. *J. Instn Struct. Engrs*, 1971, Sept.
5. DEPARTMENT OF TRANSPORT. *UK standard bridges*. HMSO, London, 1979.

8

Easing articulation restraint:
sympathetic creep and partial fixity

Fig. 8.1. Fiveways Interchange flyovers, Hendon, London

8.1. Bridge articulation

Bridge articulation is defined as the mechanism which accommodates the movements and flexures in all directions of the deck of the structure under consideration—a state of mobility which is ever-present under such varied influences as temperature, wind, settlement, the mechanisms of concrete drying, wetting and creep, plus the effects of differentials of these influences. In addition there are also prestressing and formwork movements (mainly occurring during construction), and the effects of traffic and, occasionally, earthquakes.

The articulation mechanism is familiar as a system of joints plus an array of bearings inserted between the deck and the pier and abutment substructures (Fig. 8.1). The associated deck-spanning arrangement which is closely tied to the articulation system, may be simply supported, continuous, or cantilever and drop-in span, or an appropriate combination.

The ideal articulation system will adequately cover all movements and rotations of the bridge or flyover considered and will additionally achieve the following desirable objectives.

First, it will minimise the number of deck joints and bearings, all with benefit to deck riding quality, maintenance, bridge appearance and both superstructure and substructure costs. These benefits are covered in chapters 2 and 11.

Second, the ideal articulation system will offer the least resistance to superstructure movements and rotations consistent with stability, with consequent savings in substructures, which must resist these movement restraint forces in addition to the deck horizontal forces arising from traffic braking and traction, wind and, where appropriate, earthquake. This benefit is covered in the current chapter, which describes bridge movements and restraints to movements, and how most of the restraints can be minimised to advantage.

Some attention is also paid to shrinkage movements within concrete decks, which pose their own problems.

8.2. Bridge movements

Bridge movements to be accommodated by the designer are specified for the UK by the DTp.[1] Some comparison of the approximate range of these movements is given in Table 8.1.

Besides the usual temperature and settlement movements common to all types of deck, it is seen that concrete possesses its own extra movements due to shrinkage, creep and prestressing. In addition, some movements can occur due to formwork settlement. Concrete also features a unique beneficial load-relieving movement, sympathetic creep, which is particularly useful in concrete substructures.

The effects of these movements peculiar to concrete are described below under concrete shrinkage, formwork settlement and sympathetic creep.

Table 8.1. Typical bridge deck movements

Cause of movement	Typical strains
1. Concrete setting heating and cooling	$\begin{cases} \text{Summer } 250 \times 10^{-6} \\ \text{Winter } 180 \times 10^{-6} \end{cases}$
2. Concrete shrinkage due to drying out	100×10^{-6}
3. Concrete prestressing	600×10^{-6}
4. Concrete creep	1000×10^{-6}
5. Temperature range concrete	500×10^{-6}
6. Temperature range steel	800×10^{-6}

Concrete shrinkage

As shown in Table 8.1, concrete shrinkage is made up of two distinct mechanisms, long term drying shrinkage and short term early thermal shrinkage. The dominant mechanism is early thermal shrinkage, which was elaborated upon by Hughes as early as 1968.[2] Guidance on designing concrete to resist the effects of restrained early thermal shrinkage came from DTp in 1987.[3]

Early thermal shrinkage movements are inevitable in all concrete members because of the heat of hydration of the cement generated in concrete during mixing and placement, which then rapidly cools during setting. This cooling can amount to over 30°C in a UK concreting operation during summer, causing early concrete thermal contraction of over 300 microstrain. This occurs at a time when the concrete is hardly set and weak in strength. Any restraint to this thermal contraction can readily cause cracking in the concrete —the restrained early thermal shrinkage cracking referred to in sections 8.3 (under 'Adjacent element restraint') and 11.4 (under 'Design to minimise restrained early thermal shrinkage cracking').

This early thermal contraction used to be lumped in with long term drying movement under the general heading 'shrinkage'. However, it is now accepted that for a typical concrete member exposed to the UK climate, true drying shrinkage is often under 100 microstrain. This is relatively insignificant compared with the early thermal shrinkage, besides which it accumulates on a much more mature and stronger concrete which is better able to resist any tensile effects of restraint.

Formwork settlement

Temporary support movement can be significant, particularly during staged construction, where a previous stage concrete has hardened on the formwork and a further heavy stage of concrete is added. It often happens that the first stage concrete is stiffer than the scaffolding or gantry support and most of the second stage load is carried in bending by the first stage, sometimes sufficient to cause premature cracking.

The two large in situ prestressed concrete segmental box deck flyovers constructed over heavy traffic using cantilevering-out techniques at Staples Corner, North London (Fig. 8.2), referred to in section 4.3, posed major problems related to just such movements. In the cantilevering-out (Figs 4.6

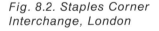

Fig. 8.2. Staples Corner Interchange, London

and 4.7), the temporary support gantry was not as stiff as the lower first stage projecting slab and hence there was heavy bending carried by this first stage slab as the second stage was poured. The bending caused cracking in the lower first stage slab in the first completed stage pour. The problem was resolved for following pours by formation of a temporary joint through the projecting slab, which was filled as the second stage was poured, thus temporarily eliminating the projecting slab stiffness and transferring all the second stage load to the support gantry.

After this it was required to close the central sections between the near half span cantilevers (Fig. 4.8). These cantilevers tended to move up and down as much as 30 mm during a daily temperature cycle and would have disturbed the freshly setting central concrete by vertical movement and, more particularly, rotation. A carefully phased construction sequence was required, involving prestressed connections across temporary construction gaps between cantilevers and the central pour.

Another bridge which was affected by temporary support movements was the river bridge of Figs 3.27 and 8.3. In this case the 24 m mid-section of the 42 m central span of the three-span continuous reinforced concrete voided slab deck was cast on a temporary Bailey bridge supported from the river bed. During the pouring of this mid-section concrete, the construction joint between it and the already cast 8 m and 10 m cantilevers had to accommodate a lot of disturbance. This comprised not only the vertical movements and rotations of the cantilever ends due to daily differential temperature but also

Fig. 8.3. Construction joint cracking, River Loughor bridge

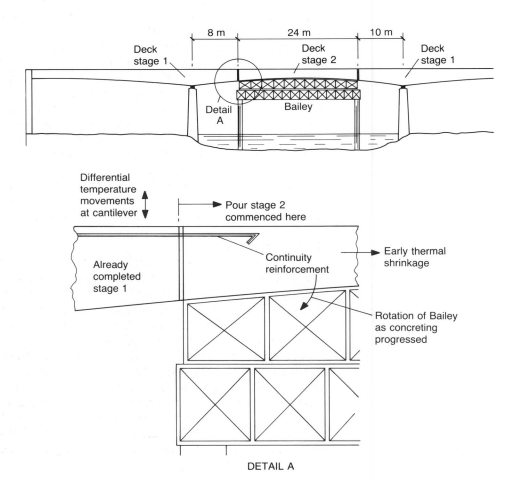

Fig. 8.4. Repair of V-pier cracking

the end flexural rotations of the Bailey supports as the mid-section concrete was poured. In addition, early thermal contractions of the mid-section were restrained by the end cantilevers.

As a consequence, the construction joints opened up, leaving the mid-section more or less hanging off the top continuity reinforcement bars connecting across the joint. Extensive epoxy compound grouting was required to restore the structural integrity of the deck.

The problems would have been overcome by pouring the mid-section slab from the centre-line using two symmetrical pouring faces, eventually finishing against both construction joints during the early morning, when differential temperature bending of the cantilevers was at a minimum and there was no more Bailey support rotation to accommodate.

Scaffolding movement during concreting can also cause cracking at the crutch of V-piers unless very rigid scaffolding is used. Fig. 8.4 shows repairs to a pier which suffered this form of cracking.

Sympathetic creep

Sympathetic creep movement is much more benevolent to the bridge designer than the image such terminology might arouse. It means that if a bridge deck is subjected to long term movement which pulls over a hinged or monolithically connected concrete pier, creep of this pier will occur in sympathy with the deck movement, greatly reducing the loads and moments set up in the pier and its foundation.

Figure 8.5 shows such a concrete deck attached to a fixed base concrete pier via a steel hinged bearing. The sudden imposition of a deck movement will create a shear force and bending on the pier in relation to its stiffness, based on the instantaneous concrete modulus of elasticity. However, as sympathetic creep occurs in the pier concrete, the shear and bending will reduce by a factor of about $1/2\theta$, where θ is the creep coefficient.[4,5] For European conditions, θ may vary between 1·5 and 2·5, giving large reduction factors, between 0·33 and 0·2.

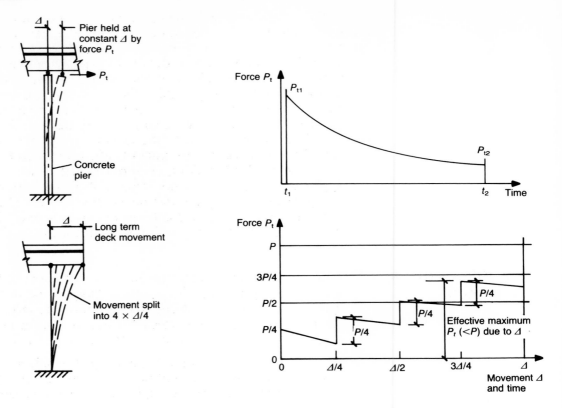

Fig. 8.5. Sympathetic creep

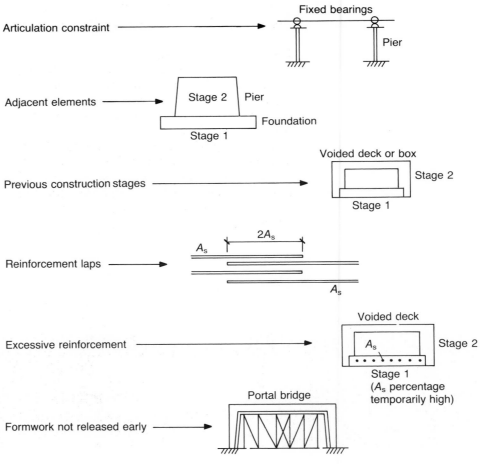

Fig. 8.6. Restraints to movement

This creep due to sudden imposition of movement is of no benefit as the full instantaneous loading must be applied to the pier anyway, before beneficial sympathetic creep reductions take place. However, where the movement is applied long term, as with deck shrinkage, creep and seasonal temperature movements, considerable pier load reduction can be gained. This is crudely illustrated in Fig. 8.5 by splitting the long term deck movement into, say, four suddenly applied movements at quarter-life intervals, each attracting its own quarter of the instantaneous shear and bending in the pier. The separation into four loading elements shows how sympathetic creep can occur and considerably lessen the maximum loading attracted to the pier at any time.

The actual load build-up is more complex as the imposed movement application is continuous, not stepped. Also, the pier stiffness characteristics change as the concrete matures and possibly cracks. The final reduction factor of the imposed slow movement is generally accepted as being greater than the sudden movement reduction factor, as defined above.[5]

8.3. Restraints to movement

With all the additional movements to which concrete bridges are subject, it will be no surprise to learn that an embuggeration factor operates to ensure that concrete bridge construction is also prone to more restraint factors than other construction forms. Restraint causes tension in the moving concrete element, which of course can lead to cracking. The factors are

(*a*) articulation constraint, including skew effects
(*b*) adjacent elements and previous construction stages
(*c*) excessive reinforcement, including reinforcement laps
(*d*) formwork restraint.

These factors are shown in Fig. 8.6 and some examples are given below.

Articulation constraint

A lot of motorway bridges, particularly in the 1950s and early 1960s, seemed to offer as much resistance as possible to free deck movement by inducing more articulation constraint than was necessary. This resistance had to be paid for in increased pier, abutment and associated foundation dimensions and reinforcement.

Two bridges on the early sections of the M4 suffered from this excessive constraint due to the use of hinged rather than movement bearings at the tops of the support piers. Not only was there needless expense on the substructures, but the bridge decks also exhibited odd movement characteristics.

One of these bridges was a heavily skewed four-span overbridge (Fig. 8.7) which rotated in plan when subjected to longitudinal movements caused by

Fig. 8.7. M4 skew over-bridge, Gloucestershire

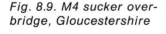

SECTION

*Fig. 8.8. Rotation of M4
skew overbridge
(S = R tan α; θ =
(Δl/l) tan α)*

prestressing and temperature. This arose because of the very large differences in the transverse and longitudinal stiffnesses of the hinged skew piers (Fig. 8.8). The rotation movement required expansion gaps extended around the deck ends at the bankseats.

The other bridge featured a variable depth three-span overbridge (Fig. 8.9) which was prestressed in two stages. The first stage released the self weight of the deck and caused support rotations sufficient to deflect the tops of the piers outwards, rather than in the expected inwards direction to match the prestressing movement.

Adjacent elements

Further forms of restraint to concrete movements arise within the structural elements themselves. The restraint offered to shrinkage of an in situ concrete deck slab by the underlying and supporting beam is a well known feature of

*Fig. 8.9. M4 sucker over-
bridge, Gloucestershire*

composite construction. However, it is not always realised that a wall pier poured on to an underlying and supporting foundation slab undergoes much the same composite action restraint and is liable to crack. Nor is it always realised that staged pouring of a voided or box section concrete deck slab again involves composite action, with restraint cracking likely in the last poured stage.

One variety of restrained movement crack that is particularly important is the 'locked-in' crack in prestressed concrete work. The progressively canti-levered segments of the flyovers constructed at Staples Corner, mentioned earlier, had to be stressed as early as possible and mixes with high cement content, and inevitably high heat generation at pouring, were required. The box segments were poured in two principal stages, bottom flange followed by webs plus top flange. This involved the early concrete setting thermal movement referred to earlier, and led to some web cracking, caused by the restraint offered to the rapidly cooling second stage pour by the relatively mature first stage (Fig. 8.10). Some of the large cracks, being locked in by the non-cracked adjacent bottom flange, would obviously never close under prestress. What gave cause for concern was that the ideal design prestress shown would change because the web crack closure had to take place before prestress across the crack depth could be established. The flanges would gain prestress, but webs became deficient in prestress in the high shear locations near the pier.

Fig. 8.10. Restrained early thermal cracking in staged box girder con-struction

In the event, it became necessary to undertake grouting of all cracks above 0·2 mm. In later pours, further reinforcing steel was added in the webs to

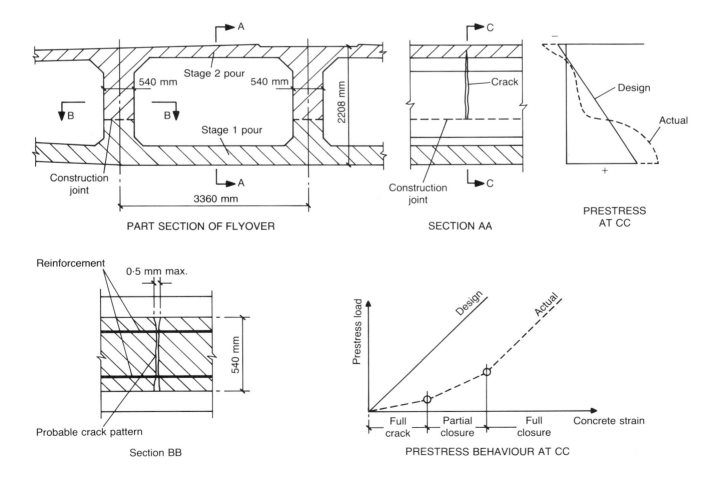

control the web cracking widths to acceptable limits. The only other way to prevent the differential straining would have been to undertake extensive mix cooling techniques or change to difficult one-stage pouring.

Such locked-in cracks can occur in reinforced concrete construction, but are generally not structurally dangerous—after all, reinforced concrete design assumes cracking over at least half the member depth. Nevertheless, some control is necessary for surface cracks from the point of view of appearance and possible corrosion.

Excessive reinforcement

Further restraint to free concrete movement is offered by the embedded reinforcement and, paradoxically, the greater the percentage, the more liable is the concrete to crack. Various codes usually provide upper limits on percentages of reinforcement to guard against this type of cracking. Nevertheless, such large percentages can occur locally by careless detailing of laps (i.e. insufficient stagger), and during staged construction.

Instances of this latter phenomenon can be found in rectangular voided reinforced concrete construction, where the base slab section is poured before the void formers are set up and the remaining webs and top slab of the deck are completed. The base slab contains most of the main longitudinal bending reinforcement, and what could be merely $1\frac{1}{2}\%$ of the whole section is perhaps over 5% of this first stage element. Such a high percentage will inevitably lead to through-cracking of the base slab, cracking which will be locked in by the poured second stage. When the soffit formwork is stripped, some trapped second stage pour water usually finds its way out via this cracking. Fortunately, the cracking is usually well below the permitted width values, and eventually

Fig. 8.11. CCI unit

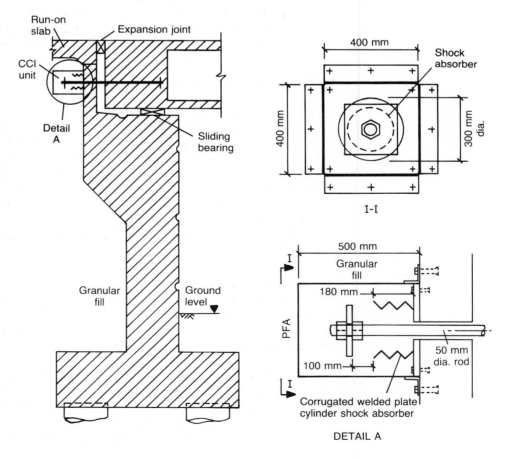

dries out. To avoid this problem it is necessary to use one-stage concreting, but this procedure can present its own problems (see section 3.8).

8.4. Minimising articulation restraint

Dissatisfaction with the intricacies of articulation restraint, described in section 8.3, led to a particular flyover project (Fig. 8.1) where so much restraint to movement was removed that the structure almost became a mechanism. This was accomplished by providing hinged bearings at the top and bottom of all piers, except at the central pier, where base fixity was provided. It was recognised that if any pier was removed by accident (or design) there could be a progressive collapse of the deck. A unique safety device was provided at each abutment to guard against such an eventuality. Known as a CCI unit (Fig. 8.11), the device took the form of a hook between deck and abutment which would come into operation as the progressive collapse threatened to pull the deck off the abutment bearing shelf. If the deck moved the other way, the strengthened abutment ballast wall would offer restraint. CCI meant Catastrophic Collapse Inhibitor, by the way!

Not all structures can be designed to move as freely as the flyover described and inevitably there are cases where deck articulation must be absorbed by piers built in to the deck. However, resistance can be acceptably reduced by adopting several design procedures

(*a*) reducing the 'free' deck movements by utilising the restraint offered by deck reinforcement

(*b*) isolating the long term shrinkage, creep and seasonal temperature movements in the deck and associating with sympathetic creep movements in any affected piers

(*c*) having no pier 'fully fixed' at its base: the base itself rotates under bending, due to either differential soil or pile movements; also, the theory of elasticity defines additional local rotations in the base adjacent to the pier wall under bending.

These three procedures are described below.

Using deck reinforcement restraint

In reinforced concrete decks or composite decks with reinforced concrete deck slabs, the deck reinforcement acts as significant restraint to temperature and shrinkage movements. Not only is the overall deck movement reduced, but this effect is enhanced for simply supported spans by the greater differential restraint offered at the soffit. This is where the main reinforcement is located, as is the bearing attachment to the piers and abutments, where the deck movements are transmitted.

Any cracking in the soffit also assists in reducing the deck movements transmitted to the piers.

Using sympathetic creep

Having taken advantage of any deck reinforcement restraint available, the effects of the deck movements to be applied through the bearings to generate forces in the deck supports can be further reduced by breaking down the movements into short term and long term and applying appropriate stiffnesses to the piers.

In general, the main short term movement is that due to the maximum daily temperature range, which is no more than half of the maximum long term temperature range specified in BS 5400. Reference should be made to Emerson's[6] work in this field.

Other short term movements which can arise are due to in situ concrete deck early thermal shrinkage and prestressing. However, these should be restricted to decks having small area, as larger decks will generally be poured or prestressed in stages separated by several days, if not weeks, giving total movements intermediate between short and long term.

Long term movements causing pier and abutment forces can be considered as the remainder of the BS 5400 specified temperature range, shrinkage and creep.

The total movements imparted to the substructure can then be applied to stiffnesses appropriate to the long and short term elements. Normal modulus of elasticity is used for the short term movements and a modulus reduced by sympathetic creep of the piers applied to the long term movements.

In normal circumstances, it is appropriate enough to take a 50% reduced modulus for the long term movements. The resulting overall reduction in movement forces on the substructure depends on the circumstances appropriate to each movement, but can range between 20% and 50%.

Using partial base fixity

The forces and moments due to deck movements applied to piers are generally calculated on the basis of pier fixity. In reality there is no such thing, as both the foundation supporting the pier and the monolithic connection of the pier to the foundation can rotate under applied moment to give a pier which is only partially fixed. This reduces the pier stiffness, which in turn reduces the applied loads and moments arising from deck movements.

As early as 1960, Leonhardt[7] provided graphs relating pier partial fixity factors to the foundation modulus and width of the supporting spread footings. The curves indicated that the combination of a narrow foundation on soil with a high modulus of reaction meant a pier base more pinned than fixed, with related reductions in deck movement forces and moments.

Using load–strain curves for piles it is also possible to calculate the base partial fixity under moments induced by deck movement in the case of piled supports.

In 1970, Lee[8] used the classical elasticity equations listed by Roark[9] to show that the elasticity of the monolithic connection between the pier base and its foundation gave extra deflection at the pier top under forces and moments applied at that level. This again reduces the effective pier stiffness under an imposed deflection, with associated reductions in pier loading. Lee showed that for typical leaf piers used on road bridges the stiffness reduction due to the connection elasticity could amount to 20–40%.

Fig. 8.12. M11 under-bridge, Woodford, London

Fig. 8.13 (above). M11 overbridge

Fig. 8.14 (right). Vehicle impact protection to columns of A23 flyover

8.5. Two bridge examples

Not only can the design techniques described in section 8.4 be used to reduce pier and foundation sizes, but also they permit the use of built-in piers, with savings in the purchase and maintenance costs of pier bearings.

Figure 8.12 shows a wide urban underbridge which featured V piers built-in to both the foundations and the reinforced concrete deck slab. Pier stiffness reductions due to connection elasticity were gained at the deck and foundation junctions.

The standard minimum maintenance M11 overbridge shown in Fig. 8.13 used simple rubber strip hinges at the top of the fixed central pier, with the outer piers built in top and bottom. The stiffness of these outer piers was further reduced by using a cluster of slender circular columns. Current pier impact requirements would require extra protection of the column, as shown in Fig. 8.14.

8.6. References

1. DEPARTMENT OF TRANSPORT. *Standard highway loadings.* HMSO, London, 1990, DTp Technical Memorandum BE1/77.
2. HUGHES. Shrinkage and thermal cracking in a reinforced concrete retaining wall. *Proc. Instn. Civ. Engrs*, 1968, Jan.
3. Department of Transport. *Early thermal cracking of concrete.* HMSO, London, 1987, DTp Departmental Standard BD28/87.
4. NEVILLE *et al. Creep of plain and structural concrete.* Construction Press, London, 1983.
5. RUSCH *et al. Creep and shrinkage.* Springer, New York, 1983.
6. EMERSON. *Extreme values of bridge temperatures for design purposes.* Transport and Road Research Laboratory, Crowthorne, 1976, report LR744.

7. LEONHARDT. Problems of supporting elevated road bridges. *Beton Stahlbeton-bau*, 1960, June.
8. LEE. *The theory and practice of bearings and expansion joints for bridges*. Cement and Concrete Association, London, 1971.
9. ROARK. *Formulas for stress and strain*. McGraw-Hill, New York.

Articulation of decks curved in plan:
guiding movement around the curve

*Fig. 9.1. Bray Viaduct,
North Devon*

9.1. Classical curved deck articulation

A bridge deck significantly curved in plan (Fig. 9.1) exhibits more complex movements and flexures than the generally plan-straight structures described in chapter 8.

Figure 9.2 shows the typical temperature expansion movement of a continuous plan-circular deck fixed in location by a hinged bearing at end A and supported friction-free at end B. The original radius R increases to $R(1 + \alpha t)$, where t is temperature rise and α is coefficient of linear temperature expansion of the deck. B moves to B_1 and it can be shown that B_1 lies on the chord line AB, length L, and that the expansion length $BB_1 = L\alpha t$. The reverse situation occurs with temperature contraction.

The principles of the ideal articulation system defined in section 8.1 still apply and are included in the classical curved deck articulation concept defined in early structural engineering textbooks. This articulation concept, still observed in modern bridge design, uses continuous multi-span decks and offers the least resistance to deck movements and rotations.

Figure 9.3 shows a typical curved continuous four-span deck ABCD supported on abutments at A and D and piers at B and C, all aligned radially to the centre-line curve of the deck. The deck is located by a spherically hinged bearing at A and pairs of sliding or roller bearings at B, C and D. The classical concept requires that the movement bearings at B, C and D should be aligned at right angles to their relative chords BA, CA and DA respectively. As a result, expansion or contraction movements and the generated bearing frictions are aligned with the respective chords and during, say, temperature expansion, B moves to B_1, C to C_1, D to D_1 and so on.

The bearing friction forces generated at supports B, C and D all align with and are resisted at the hinge joint A, an articulation offering the least resistance to deck movements and rotations and the least plan bending.

Each bearing on each pier must be aligned on its own chord, requiring slightly non-parallel settings of the bearings on top of each pier or end abutment. It can be shown that the deck lateral movement between bearing centres exactly matches the lateral divergence or convergence movements of the two bearings at each support during temperature rise or fall, generating no extra articulation forces.

However, in practice there would be a temperature differential between the deck and the support pier or free end abutments, principally because of the shelter from the sun's radiant heat provided by the deck. This means that the design range of temperature for the deck would be less at the top of each support pier or abutment, and that transverse movements of these supports and their bearings would be correspondingly less. This in turn would cause a tendency for differential movement between the upper and lower bearing plates at each bearing.

The temperature differential would not be great, probably less than a $\pm 5°C$ maximum, representing very small free differential movement. This would be resisted by the line frictions between bearing rollers and the top and bottom plates, or in transverse friction between sliding plate bearings, probably sufficient to prevent this small movement tendency. Even if slip did occur, it would probably be less than ± 0.1 mm, readily absorbed in the fit-up tolerances of the bearings.

The classical articulation concept works well with shallow curvatures. However, difficulties increasingly arise as the angle θ turned through by the deck increases. As indicated in Fig. 9.3, the free end of the deck moves across bearings which are skewed at an average angle of $\theta/2$ to the abutment shelf. Thus, for an expansion or contraction of the deck at the free-end expansion joint of $\pm e$, the square expansion joint moves laterally $\pm e \sin \theta/2$. For the extreme case of a curved flyover turning through a right angle this means that

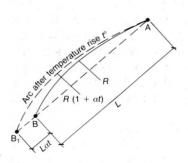

Fig. 9.2. Free temperature expansion of curved arc hinged at one end

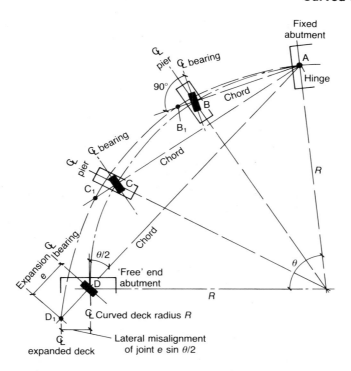

Fig. 9.3. Classical articulation of curved viaduct

the lateral movements at the expansion joint are as much as the longitudinal movements. The problem that arises is that the deck kerbs and parapets will misalign with the kerbs and parapets on the abutment side of the joint as the deck moves.

Kerbs and parapets misaligned by several centimetres are dangerous to traffic and, in the case of parapets, are not permitted in the relevant parapet code. The designer is therefore faced with providing a complex kerb and parapet transition arrangement or changing the deck articulation from classical to guided.

One further possible disadvantage of the classical articulation lies in the bearing chorded alignments, which generally require construction of the deck sequentially from the hinged end and do not readily permit the builder to use other sequences. If this proves to be a problem, the guided articulation system can again provide a useful substitution for the classical articulation system.

9.2. Guided curved deck articulation

It would be possible to modify the classical articulation shown in Fig. 9.3 by setting the two bearings D_1 and D_2 radial to the curve and in line with each other on the abutment bearing shelf. With side restraints to these bearings, the end of the deck could be guided in line with the curved centre-line to generate no transverse movements at the expansion joint and no kerb and parapet misalignments during movement. However, the guided end of the deck would suffer considerable horizontal bending, and large transverse forces would be generated by the bearing guides.

Rather than attempting to guide the moving deck into line in one large redirecting deflection at the free end, it is far better to guide the moving deck around and in line with its own curve in small increments using guided bearings at each pier, besides at the free end abutment.

Figure 9.4 shows the same deck and substructure as in Fig. 9.3, but this time the bearings are guided and set to move tangentially to the deck, in line with

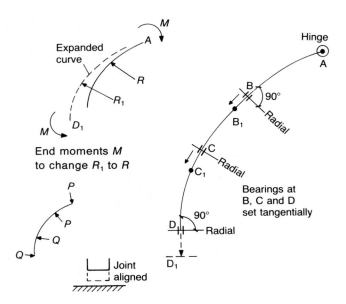

Fig. 9.4. Guided articula-
tion of curved viaduct

and on the centre-lines of the radial piers and free abutment. The guidance given by the bearings to the moving deck sets up radial forces at the guides, which in turn bend the deck horizontally to counter the change of deck horizontal radius caused by temperature rise or fall.

The value of these radial reactions generated by a rise in temperature of t can be estimated by applying end moments M to the curved deck equivalent to $EI/R\alpha t$, where E and I are the modulus of elasticity and horizontal bending stiffness respectively of the deck and $R\alpha t$ is as defined in section 9.1.

The approximate reactions are then obtained by dividing M by the end spans L, applied at the abutments and in the opposing direction at the penultimate piers. More accurate reactions are obtained using a plane-frame computer program, which will also include the extra longitudinal friction generated by the guides.

The radial reactions are generally maximum at the penultimate piers, and the approximate value of $EI/R\alpha tL$ indicates that the reactions and horizontal bending increase as deck horizontal bending stiffness increases and the deck curvature radius decreases. However, for normal road curvatures and two-lane or three-lane roads, the radial reactions and bending effects are not very significant. Dual two-lane or three-lane roads would generally increase stiffnesses nearly eightfold and give rise to very significant radial reactions and bending—hence the value of splitting the deck into two half-deck superstructures on these occasions.

The main value of guided articulation lies in the resulting tangential movements at the free end expansion joint and undoubtedly warrants the small extra radial forces on the piers and abutments plus some small additional horizontal deck bending. However, in certain circumstances, described in section 9.3, it can prove invaluable in giving the builder more flexibility in his method of construction.

Guided articulation has been used on curved bridges and flyovers since the early 1960s and two examples are shown in Figs 9.5 and 9.6.

9.3. Bray Viaduct

Bray Viaduct, built to carry the North Devon Link Road (Fig. 9.1), received high recommendation in the Concrete Society Awards of 1990 for its designers

*Fig. 9.5 (right). Churchill
Way flyovers, Liverpool*

*Fig. 9.6 (below). Docklands
Light Railway viaducts,
London*

Gifford/Graham.[1] For part of its length the link road follows a section of the abandoned Devon and Somerset Railway, which included five high piers of the old curved in plan railway viaduct crossing the Bray valley. It was decided to retain these piers, in conjunction with three new piers, to support a new continuous nine-span reinforced concrete slab bridge, similarly curved in plan.

The bridge, which was some 280 m long and curved through 22°, was designed using the classical articulation arrangement, with the twin roller bearings on each pier and free west end abutment aligned to move along chords emanating from the single central hinged fixed bearing at the east end.

As stated earlier, the classical articulation arrangement would generally only have permitted sequential building from the hinged east end abutment. Any attempt to build the deck from another temporarily hinged fixed location, say from a pier or from the free west abutment, would have been fraught with difficulties which could have proved expensive in time and money.

When the contract was let, such a situation arose, and the contractor found that access and other difficulties dictated building sequentially from the 'wrong', west end, abutment.

This meant that, first, the deck would have to be temporarily fixed at this new, west end, location. This could be done by fixing the moving bearings at the location during deck construction and releasing them in a planned and controlled sequence after deck completion.

Second, during the deck construction, the remaining moving bearings would have to be set to an alignment differing from that finally required, each aimed at the temporarily fixed moving bearings at the west end. On completion, these bearings would have to be swivelled back to the final alignments. This would be a lengthy operation involving a complex sequence at each support of unloading the bearings by vertical jacking, releasing the fixing bolts, realigning the bearings, refixing the bolts and then reloading by jacking. There was another possible method using temporary moving bearings for deck construction. Using this, the permanent bearings would not have needed any temporary realignment, but complex staged load transfers from the temporary to the permanent bearings would still have been required. In addition, there would have been the extra cost of these temporary bearings.

Third, with the temporary fixity located at the free expansion joint west end of the deck, the realigned moving bearings near the east end would not have had enough movement capacity during deck construction.

It was fortunate that analysis indicated that very little extra force would be applied to the sensitive original masonry-clad piers by changing the articulation to guided, with the bearings set to run tangentially and in line with the radial piers and free abutment. The minor changes in the articulation system forces required no strengthening of the piers nor of the bearings and their guides.

The contractor only needed to change the originally designed alignments when setting the bearings on the piers and west abutment. He was then able to sequentially construct the deck from the temporarily fixed west end with none of the problems which would have been associated with the original classical articulation.

9.4. Reference

1. HOLLINGHURST. The Bray Viaduct reincarnation. *J. Instn Highw. Transpn*, 1988, June.

10

Shock transmission units: *sharing horizontal loads on substructures*

Fig. 10.1. 50 t shock transmission unit

10.1. What is a shock transmission unit?

A shock transmission unit (STU) is a special mechanism joining separate structures or separate elements of structures. The unique property of the STU is that it permits slow long term movements between the structures with negligible resistance, yet is capable of acting temporarily as a rigid link between the structures, transmitting short-duration shock or impact forces.

This means that a series of structures or structural elements subject to long term separation movements, such as temperature expansions or contractions, can be linked together with STUs to beneficially share among them short-duration dynamic loads applied to any one of the structures or structural elements. With, say, five equal-stiffness structures, a dynamic load applied randomly to any one structure will be resisted equally by five structures. This leads to a reduction of dynamic loading on each structure support system of 80%. In general, it is not possible to link the structures permanently together with simple rigid structural elements because large extra forces would be generated by the restraint to long term separation movements.

STUs have found a number of important applications in all types of engineering over the years. Hitherto, the STU was a relatively complex oil-filled or gas-filled device with a high first cost and a continuing need for regular and expensive maintenance and adjustment. This tended to limit the number of applications of this very useful mechanism.

Nevertheless, the 5 km long Oosterschelde Bridge, completed in Holland in 1965, used STUs extensively. Units of up to 180 t capacity were mounted under the steel-comb movement joints located in the centre of the 90 m span concrete box girder decks. Their purpose was 'to counteract the joint movements [due to temperature] with only minimal resistance'. Similar oil-filled STUs were used on the approach spans to the Kingston Bridge, completed in Glasgow in 1970.[1]

Around this time a new type of STU was invented. A unique chemical compound of boron-filled dimethyl syloxane, known as silicone putty, was developed in America in the 1960s and used in the space exploration programme. It offered special thixotropic properties, readily deforming under slowly applied pressure but acting as a rigid body under impact. John Chafe and the late Reg Mander, both engineers with the then UK Ministry of Transport, realised that the new material was eminently suited to STUs, offering a better and simpler filler material than the special oils and gases then in use. They developed and patented[2] an STU using the new silicone putty, initially targetted for use in bridges. Using only one moving part, it offered structural designers a low-cost, robust and minimum-maintenance STU for the first time.

After some negotiations, the then UK National Research and Development Corporation granted a licence to Messrs Colebrand to market and further develop the Chafe–Mander STU.

Fig. 10.2. New silicone putty 50 t STU

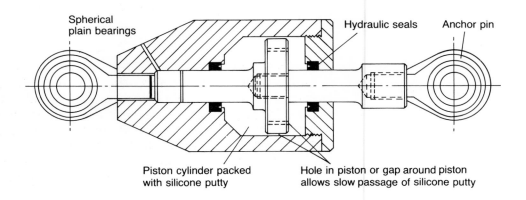

Spherical plain bearings   Hydraulic seals   Anchor pin

Piston cylinder packed with silicone putty

Hole in piston or gap around piston allows slow passage of silicone putty

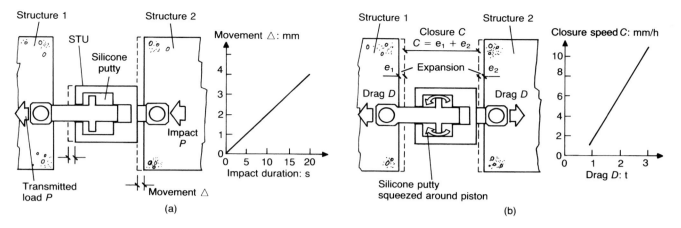

Fig. 10.3. STU force–movement characteristics: (a) short term impact transmission; (b) long term movement (expansion shown)

The typical 50 t capacity unit illustrated in Figs 10.1 and 10.2 uses a steel cylinder containing a loose-fitting piston fixed to a transmission rod, the void around the rod being filled with the silicone putty. The unit is attached to the two separate structures or structural elements by fixing eyes located on the cylinder at one end and the transmission rod at the other. The transmission rod passes through the entire length of the cylinder so that the volume of the cylinder and the silicone putty filler remains constant at all piston positions. Under slow movement between the structures the putty is squeezed through the clearance gap around the piston, or a hole through the piston, and displaced from one end of the cylinder to the other, generating only small 'drag' forces between the structures.

When a short-duration impact is applied to one structure, there is negligible movement of the piston (Fig. 10.3) and the impact tensile or compressive force is passed along the load path of transmission rod/piston head/silicone putty/cylinder to the second structure. The rating of the unit defines the maximum impact force which can be transmitted, and the length of the transmission rod can be varied to suit the expected long term axial movements between the fixing eyes attached to the separate structures.

STUs of 25–50 t capacity are particularly compact, lightweight and economic, and if larger impact forces have to be catered for it usually is best to provide groups of the smaller units.

The new STU has been designed primarily to function in a horizontal position. However, it can be readily adapted for vertical movement and impact transmission by incorporation of an internal spring to return the piston to the neutral position.

For all practical purposes the unique thixotropic properties of the silicone putty do not vary significantly through a wide temperature range. Thus the new STU can be relied on to perform consistently under most climatic conditions.

10.2. Use of the STU in bridges

The new STU offers the bridge designer a robust, low-cost and virtually maintenance-free mechanism which can be simply attached between separate structures or structural elements which are subject to long term movement. The STU provides the following characteristics, which can be used to advantage in structural design: first, it freely expands and contracts in response to the long term movements of the structures or structural elements, generating virtually no restraint to these movements; and secondly, it acts as a temporary fixed link between the structures or structural elements to beneficially transmit, transfer or share applied short-duration impact or shock loads for the duration of these forces.

Thus the new STU can be applied to structures subject to

(*a*)   significant long term movements, such as temperature or differential-temperature expansions and contractions, settlement, concrete shrinkage and creep

(*b*)   significant short-duration shock or impact loadings, such as road or rail vehicle traction, braking, centrifugal force, nosing, accidental impact and, in various parts of the world, earthquake loading.

Probably the most effective use of the new STU is in bridging, the application originally targeted by the Ministry of Transport and the Transport and Road Research Laboratory. The design economies possible and some recent examples are described in the next sections.

10.3. Design of multi-span bridge substructures

Multi-span bridge or viaduct deck superstructures are supported on substructures formed of a series of piers and abutments. Each substructure must be designed to cater for not only the vertical loads due to the weight of the supported superstructures and the road or rail traffic carried, but also the dynamic short-duration horizontal loads arising from that traffic and from long-duration deck movements.

Ideally, these horizontal loads would be shared out among all the substructure piers and abutments to provide the optimum and most economic design by attaching the piers and abutments to the deck superstructure, either by building in or by using fixed bearings.

Unfortunately, as discussed in chapter 8, bridge decks are always on the move, with plan dimensional changes mainly due to temperature rise and fall. Further movements can arise due to shrinkage, prestressing and creep in concrete bridge deck superstructures.

The movements can generate very large horizontal restraint forces in an attached substructure, completely negating any benefit to be gained in sharing out the traffic horizontal loads. To avoid these large and unnecessary restraint forces, the designer inevitably detaches the deck superstructure from the substructure by inserting moving bearings offering as little resistance to movement as possible at the tops of piers and abutments. To resist the traffic and, where appropriate, earthquake horizontal loading the deck is usually attached by fixed bearings either to one abutment or to one or two central piers. Thus, the beneficial sharing of this short-duration traffic and earthquake loading is normally lost.

The use of the new STU can readily restore the advantageous sharing of short-duration horizontal load without building in any large restraint forces due to deck movement. By connection of the detached deck to the substructure, using STUs, the substructure is virtually fixed to the deck for short-duration traffic and earthquake loading, with full load-sharing. After this temporary fixity, it reverts to a detached state offering virtually no restraint to longer term deck movement.

From the curves in Fig. 10.3, it can be seen that the maximum STU restraint to deck movement is generated by the fastest long term deck movements. These occur in a typical UK bridge during the daily cycle of temperature rise and fall. For a steel deck the maximum temperature rise can be as high as 4°C/h. The maximum speed of movement is at the expansion joint, where an STU would be subjected to some 5 mm/h movement for, say, every 100 m length of expanding steel deck. A similar concrete deck would suffer around half this movement.

From the long term movement characteristics shown in Fig. 10.3, the maximum restraint, or 'drag', force generated by a 50 t STU fixed across the expansion joint of a 200 m long steel deck, moving at up to 10 mm/h, would be less than 3 t. This force is negligible in terms of deck articulation. As regards the transmission of short-duration traffic and earthquake load, individual impact load duration is unlikely to exceed 10 s, and it can be seen that a 50 t STU moves no more than 2–3 mm during this period of load transmission, acting virtually as a rigid link.

For the design of the substructures of new multi-span bridges or viaducts, the incorporation of STUs shows most advantage in three particular situations. These are described below.

New multi-span simply supported bridges

Multi-span bridges or viaducts are often made up of a series of simply supported spans rather than continuous spans. The reasons for this choice may range from an expectation of future large settlements in poor ground or areas of mining subsidence to the economic standardised use of precast beam

Fig. 10.4. Using STUs on a multi-span simply supported bridge

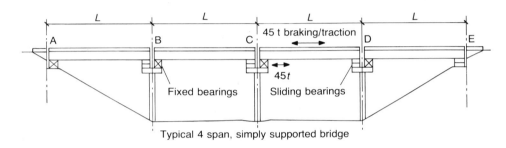

Typical 4 span, simply supported bridge

45 t traction/braking in span	Horizontal load on support: t				
	A	B	C	D	E
AB	45	—	—	—	—
BC	—	45	—	—	—
CD	—	—	45	—	—
DE	—	—	—	45	—

Total support horizontal design capacity required for traction/braking = 45 t + 45 t + 45 t + 45 t
= 180 t

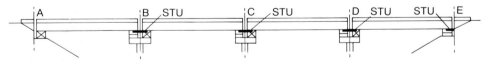

Addition of 4 STUs
(for simplicity assume equal stiffnesses at all supports)

45 t traction/braking in span	Horizontal load on support: t				
	A	B	C	D	E
AB	9	9	9	9	9
BC	9	9	9	9	
CD	9	9	9	9	9
DE	9	9	9	9	9

Total support horizontal design capacity required for traction/braking = 9 t + 9 t + 9 t + 9 t + 9 t
= 45 t

units. Whatever the virtues of the simply supported spans for the deck, the substructure will require overdesign.

A typical simply supported four-span deck is shown in Fig. 10.4. The piers under each simply supported span carry the usual fixed bearings for one span alongside free bearings for the adjacent span. This means of course that the design longitudinal traction and braking forces must be individually applied to each deck span throughout the viaduct. Main resistance is offered by the pier or bankseat carrying the fixed bearings of that particular span, with generally a small additional resistance from friction generated at the free bearings carrying that span, located over the next pier. However, clause 5.14.2.2 of BS 5400 states that free-bearing frictions 'are not applicable when calculating stabilizing forces against externally applied loads'. This means that all resistance must come from the fixed bearings.

This means that a substructure of this type, with (say) equal-stiffness bankseats and piers, has to have a total designed capacity of four times the required deck design traction and braking longitudinal loads. However, by placing four new STUs at bearing level on the free bankseat and the piers, as shown, it is possible to share out the traction and braking load acting anywhere on the deck among all three piers and both bankseats. This in turn allows significant reduction of pier and fixed bankseat sizes and foundations to give a total designed horizontal load capacity only some 25% of that required originally.

New multi-span continuous bridges

Load relief can also be used to benefit in new multi-span continuous decks. Two long viaducts designed by Kent County Council and completed in 1979 and 1982 used STUs attached to the decks at abutment shelf level to relieve the longitudinal loading on the central fixed piers, which were founded on particularly poor estuarial soils (Figs 10.5 and 10.6).

New continuous bridges in earthquake zones

The longitudinal forces generated in a bridge deck subjected to an earthquake shock are a function of the deck mass and generally result in forces well

Fig. 10.5 (left). Using STUs on a multi-span continuous viaduct, Kent

Fig. 10.6 (right). Kent viaduct

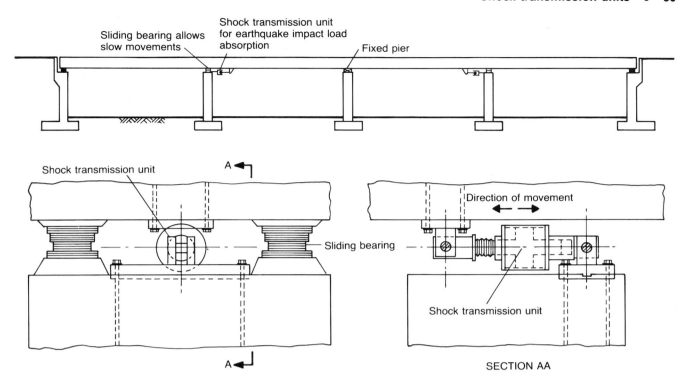

Sliding bearing allows slow movements

Shock transmission unit for earthquake impact load absorption

Fixed pier

Shock transmission unit

Sliding bearing

A

A

Direction of movement

Shock transmission unit

SECTION AA

Fig. 10.7 (above). Using STUs on flyovers in an earthquake region (note: fixed pier resists long term horizontal forces; all piers resist transient forces)

Fig. 10.8. Flyover, Kuwait

Fig. 10.9. STU on flyover, Kuwait

in excess of any design requirements for braking and traction of traffic. These large forces necessitate the development of considerable longitudinal restraint from the substructure at bearing level.

Consider a typical viaduct having a central fixed pier or a fixed abutment, and sliding, roller or rubber bearings at all other piers and abutments to accommodate deck movements. Earthquake forces on such a structure would overload the fixed pier or abutments. However, by attaching STUs on the 'free' pier and/or abutment bearing shelves (Fig. 10.7), the earthquake shock loading can be beneficially shared out between all the substructure elements. The temporary attachment to the deck can also benefit the 'free' piers, which have to cater for their own earthquake loading. For tall free piers, stability can also be improved during earthquake loading.

STUs were used in this manner on a Kuwait flyover[3] designed for earthquake loading (Figs 10.8 and 10.9).

10.4. Strengthening multi-span bridge substructures

Probably the most advantageous use of STUs is to be found in the strengthening of substructures of existing multi-span bridges.

This subject is covered in chapter 14.

10.5. Parapet STU

In part 1 of BS 6779, *Parapets for vehicle containment on highways*,[4] it is stated that STUs may be used as one of two methods for dealing with expansion joints in high containment parapets. The STU is defined as being able to transmit not less than 500 kN and to be incorporated in the joint between the top and second effective rail at as high a position as is practicable.

In general, the method has not been economically competitive with the alternative of strengthened end parapet bays adjacent to the joint. Nevertheless, some interest has been shown in the use of the method for large joint movements. The degree of force transmission required can be gauged from the testing of a non-jointed high containment parapet (Fig. 10.10).

Fig. 10.10. Testing of high-containment parapet

Fig. 10.11. Rotational STU

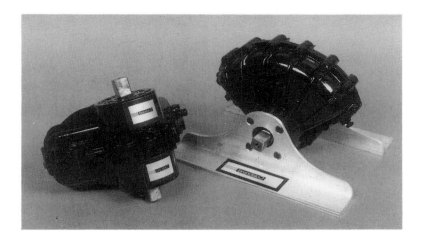

10.6. Rotational STU

The STU principle can be extended to rotational applications to provide a mechanism between two separate structures which will allow free slow-acting relative rotations but transmit bending moment and shear during fast-acting relative rotations. Fig. 10.11 shows a rotational unit which was developed for military pontoon-bridging.

The units connect each floating pontoon of the bridge and the bridging elements attached to the river banks. The slow rise and fall of the river bridge is accommodated by free rotation of the bridging element joint units. The slow individual rotations of each pontoon due to river swell and currents are similarly accommodated by free rotation of the pontoon joint units.

However, when a heavy military vehicle such as a tank drives on to the floating bridge, relative rotation between the bank and pontoon elements is minimised by the temporary fixity of the joint unit, usefully reducing the 'nose-diving' impact as the tank crossed on to the first pontoon unit. More important is the shear and moment transfer offered by the temporarily locked pontoon joint units. This allows more spread of the tank load between pontoons to the extent that the numbers of pontoon units required for a river crossing can be usefully reduced.

With an increasing interest in floating bridges for long water crossings, the rotational STU could offer highly beneficial stiffening and load spread under traffic.

10.7. References

1. FAIRHURST *et al.* The design and construction of Kingston Bridge and elevated approach roads, Glasgow. *Struct. Engr*, 1971, Jan.
2. MANDER and CHAFFE. UK patent application 13198/70, 19 Mar. 1970.
3. PRITCHARD. Shock transmission units for bridge design, construction and strengthening. *Constrn Repair*, 1989, Oct.
4. BRITISH STANDARDS INSTITUTION. *Parapets for vehicle containment on highways*. BSI, London, 1989, BS 6779, part 1, section 11.1.2.

11

Designing for durability: *resisting corrosion from road de-icing salt*

Fig. 11.1. Salt corrosion

11.1. Bridge durability

There are several important attack mechanisms which affect the durability of the bridges built of steel–concrete or of concrete considered in this book.

Steel members in composite deck structures can suffer corrosion and loss of structural integrity. However, the specification of suitable protective painting systems[1] and regular cycles of easily visible inspection and repainting when necessary can ensure durable steel members with lives in excess of the designed 120 year life, which is possibly more dependent on steel fatigue considerations. The recent introduction of enclosures[2] has added easier inspection and maintenance together with longer intervals between repainting. The use of Corten steels and high-build paint systems has also led to cost reductions in maintenance painting.

Concrete decks, formed as solid or voided slabs, as slabs composite with steel or precast concrete beams, or as in situ or precast girders of box or T beam section, can suffer from alkali–silica reaction (ASR) and carbonation. The former causes overall concrete cracking and the latter depassivation of the protective alkaline film around embedded steel reinforcement or prestressing tendons. Both mechanisms lead to corrosion of these embedments and loss of structural integrity. However, proper choice of aggregates and cements[3] can avoid ASR, which fortunately tends to be a localised phenomenon in the UK. In addition, the correct application of concrete covers to steel embedments will ensure that the slowly advancing wave of carbonation from the concrete surface should never reach the embedded steel to cause depassivation within the life of 120 years required of a UK bridge.

By far the most destructive attack mechanism is steel corrosion caused by winter road-salting operations. This can attack steel within the concrete deck slab underlying the salted road surfacing, can spread downwards to composite steel or precast concrete beams, attacking steel and any shear connectors. Or it can penetrate into the webs, bottom flanges and diaphragms of the in situ or precast box or T beam girders. It can also spread to the underlying substructure via cracks or joints in the decks or through salt-laden splash from passing traffic.

It is now very evident that the growing use of salt as a winter de-icing agent for a large proportion of the world stock of concrete bridges has caused an enormous amount of corrosion damage to embedded reinforcing or prestressing steel. The bills to repair or replace can be measured in many billions of pounds, and a lot of research effort is now being directed towards cathodic protection and even desalination of salt-damaged concrete structures. Salt is bad for our diets, so the sensible eater minimises his intake. Salt is also bad for our concrete bridges, but a similar remedy is not readily available when the demands for road de-icing arise each winter.

This chapter describes this most dominant threat to bridge durability and then offers a range of measures which can be applied during the design and detailing of new bridges to improve resistance to salt attack and hence to extend durability and minimize future maintenance.

11.2. Road salt de-icing

It is a tedious fact that most of the highly industrialised nations lie in the winter snow and ice regions of the northern hemisphere. These nations are very dependent on sophisticated highway networks which must be kept clear during winter, when the common remedy of spreading road salt for de-icing is applied.

There is no difficulty in understanding why salt-spreading has become the universal panacea. Salt is readily available, easily applied, highly efficient in ice and snow removal and relatively cheap in use.

Unfortunately, winter salt-spreading operations are inevitably followed by the melting of ice or snow, and the water run-off from the treated roads turns into a harmful sodium chloride solution. In the form of spray or run-off, this solution can damage bridges carrying or crossing the treated roads. It can corrode and weaken steel elements by direct contact, or it can penetrate the exposed faces of concrete elements, causing weakening corrosion of embedded reinforcement bars or prestressing cables, or both, in these bridges (Fig. 11.1).

In addition, the rapid heat withdrawal from salt-treated concrete surfaces can cause a sudden local surface temperature drop of up to 10°C within one minute after application (thermal shock). Where salting is repeated several times a day for protracted periods during severe winters, the shocks can cause early concrete surface cracking. This in turn can hasten surface water penetration, ice formation and the familiar freeze–thaw surface spalling and concrete disintegration.

The UK generally suffers winters which are relatively mild compared with those of some of its European neighbours and parts of North America. Consequently, the freeze–thaw phenomenon is not a great threat to most UK bridges. However, the bridge corrosion damage resulting from the winter salting of roads has become a major threat to bridge durability in the UK as in the rest of the road-salting world, possibly because of the considerable increase in the stock of potentially vulnerable reinforced and prestressed concrete bridges, together with steel–concrete composite bridges, which have dominated construction over the past three decades. In the case of the UK this has combined with some recent severe winters and a massive increase in road salting of up to 15-fold in the same period.[4] It is also possible that specification emphasis worldwide on concrete strength rather than impermeability has contributed to the apparent greater vulnerability of these more recent bridges.

To avoid salt corrosion, consideration has been given at various times to such measures as under-road heating or the spreading of urea in place of road salt. The former disappeared in the wake of energy-saving campaigns and the latter is only used sparingly in special situations because of the high cost compared with salt, the carry-over of road salt from adjacent stretches of road, and pollution of adjacent watercourses. Two such urea operations in the UK are located at the Severn and Avon crossings, where road salt corrosion threatened the box girder steel plate decking, and in the 20 km M5/M6

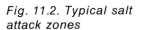

Fig. 11.2. Typical salt attack zones

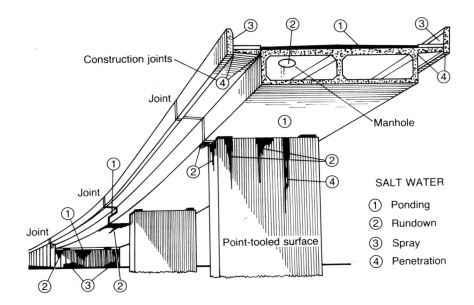

Midlands Links viaducts around Birmingham, where the concrete deck slabs and substructures are vulnerable.

In Germany, attempts have been made to reduce the quantity of salt used during winter de-icing operations by using damp salt and improved spreading techniques.

The mechanism of salt attack, the resulting corrosion and the various methods of detection and repair are summarised in a recent CIRIA publication.[5]

11.3. Typical salt attack zones

Figure 11.2 shows a typical concrete bridge unfortunate enough to be suffering from winter de-icing salt attack in all the zones subjected to ponding, rundown and direct cover penetration which are commonly met with in bridge inspections. They are listed below.

Deck slabs

The problems of salt attack on concrete deck slabs via penetration of the porous asphalt surfacing was recognised early, and different types of waterproofing membrane have been used on UK bridge decks for up to four decades. However, some membranes suffer ageing, embrittlement or loss of elasticity, and, as a consequence, local water penetration, entrapment and ponding can occur.[6] There have also been cases of bridge deck resurfacing where the existing membrane has suffered unobserved local damage. In both cases, winter de-icing salt can penetrate locally and can set up unsuspected corrosion.

Prestressed decks

Most prestressed concrete bridge decks are built of precast pre-tensioned beams composite with reinforced in situ concrete deck slabs, post-tensioned beams with composite deck slabs, or post-tensioned box or T girders, either in situ or precast. A large number of continental bridge decks and some earlier UK decks also utilise transverse post-tensioning.

The majority of the post-tensioned concrete bridge decks have been built with grouted tendons embedded in the webs or flanges. Recent inspections have revealed that ungrouted lengths of tendons near the road surfacing are

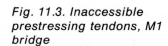

Fig. 11.3. Inaccessible prestressing tendons, M1 bridge

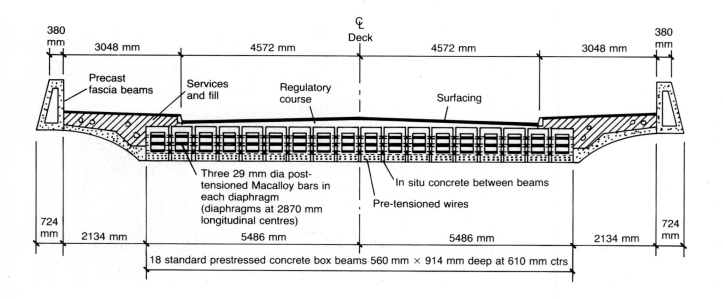

Fig. 11.4. Evidence of cor-rosion under M1 bridge

a special corrosion problem of post-tensioned decks. The hollow spaces can actually suck in moisture by air temperature differentials between void and salted deck.[7]

It is difficult to establish the extent of salt corrosion without actually viewing the prestressing cables, which can only be done by physically removing the adjacent deck concrete and the duct grout. The deck structural integrity is highly sensitive to both operations because failure can be readily triggered by notching a highly stressed tendon with any of the drills, chisels or hammers used. The Germans invented appropriate terms for this operation 'careful or delicate drilling'.[8]

Such inspections are always limited to tendons near the concrete surface and can only represent a small sampling of the overall tendon state. Most tendons are generally inaccessible, as with the tendons of the structure shown in Fig. 11.3. The pre-tensioned precast box girders were transversely pre-stressed with Macalloy bars located in the middle of the deck. There was no deck slab, only surfacing laid directly on top of a waterproofing layer. Fig. 11.4 shows the deck soffit some 25 years later, the deck stalactites and rust on the bankseat indicating that salt water has penetrated the joints between the box beams to corrode the Macalloy tendons. Worse, salt water has penetrated the box beams and lies several centimetres deep inside over the bottom flanges

Fig. 11.5. Demolition of prestressed concrete flyover, Berlin

Fig. 11.6. Demolition of prestressed concrete flyover, South Wales

containing all the pre-tensioning strands. Proper inspection of the prestressing tendons is extremely limited, the transverse bars being quite inaccessible and the box beam pre-tensioning strands requiring expensive 'delicate drilling'.

Continuous decks generally require prestressing tendons located in the deck slab or in the top flange and top of web in box girders. The tendons are close to the road surfacing receiving the de-icing salt. Having penetrated the first barrier of deck waterproofing (as stated earlier, a fairly regular occurrence), the chloride solution has not far to permeate to start corroding these tendons. The top slab or flange also suffers localised bending due to live load and the resulting transverse bending and localised longitudinal bending at crossbeams is generally resisted by reinforcement, resulting in cracking. Such cracks in the top surface greatly hasten the corrosion process. The continuous German flyover shown in Fig. 11.5 had to be demolished because of this form of salt attack. The stack of removed chopped-up tendons in the foreground exhibited heavy pitting corrosion. Another bridge with similar problems is shown being demolished in Wales (Fig. 11.6).

Deck construction joints

If salt solution can penetrate through to the top of the concrete deck, any construction joints offer a ready and rapid route for corrosion attack of reinforcement passing through the joint, due to the inevitable shrinkage cracking at the joint.

There are of course construction joints in precast prestressed concrete segmental deck construction, but, being prestressed, there is less chance of upper surface cracking allowing passage of deck salt solutions. However, where narrow jointing concrete is used it includes two construction joints and, even prestressed, these can still allow the passage of salt-laden water down the interfaces (Fig. 11.7). The 1985 Ynys-y-Gwas bridge deck collapse in Wales (Fig. 11.8) demonstrated how vulnerable these segmental beam joints can be to salt attack and how quickly the prestressing tendons crossing the joints can be corroded away with little visible warning of distress.[9]

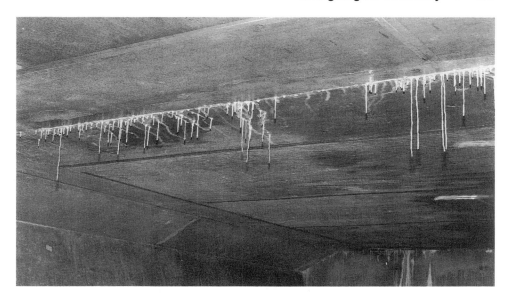

Fig. 11.7. Water penetration through deck construction joints

Fig. 11.8. Collapsed prestressed concrete bridge, South Wales

Parapet beams

Parapet beams, particularly the solid concrete P1 and P6 parapet barriers, can suffer considerable rainwater splash from traffic. In winter this can contain harmful salt. Corrosion attack is usually slow in developing, but can be particularly rapid in local areas where the shelter of overlying structures prevents the beneficial cleansing actions of rain or salt-free spray at other times of the year.

In addition, parapet beams are usually poured after the main deck has been constructed, almost inviting restrained early thermal shrinkage cracking which can speed up the corrosion process. It is for this reason that special anti-corrosion measures are specified for parapets in BS 5400 part 4, sections 4.1.1.1 and 5.8.2.

Fig. 11.9. Leaking deck expansion joints

Deck soffits

Wide decks and underpasses with long approaches can funnel salt-water spray from traffic to build up and generate a salt-laden mist under the bridge soffit. Chloride penetration and attack can result as beneficial rain-washing is again not possible. Fortunately, this form of attack is usually only found in the more severe winter conditions of places like Berlin in Germany or parts of North America.

Deck expansion joints

Most deck expansion joints leak and salt solutions from the road above can run down the vertical deck edges on to the tops of piers or abutment shelves (Fig. 11.9). These concrete surfaces are not usually waterproofed nor are they effectively cleansed by rain. Salt corrosion can occur and some of the affected zones are difficult to inspect, let alone repair. Leakage can also spread back across the top of the deck under the end of the waterproofing and across the deck soffit.

Fig. 11.10. Leaking deck half-joint

A notoriously difficult situation for inspection and access is to be found with half-joint arrangements for cantilever and drop-in span decks (Fig. 11.10). Rundown and ponding can cause corrosion not only on the bearings, but also in any underlying prestressing tendons and anchorages. Full access can be gained only by jacking up the suspended span.

A potentially dangerous combination is where the end of a prestressed beam or slab also forms the end of the deck and one side of the deck joint. The prestressing tendon anchorages lie just beneath the vertical face, protected only by a thin slab of added reinforced concrete, which is liable to crack due to restrained early thermal shrinkage. Salt penetration causing anchorage and cable corrosion could produce dangerous loss of prestress, particularly for incompletely grouted tendons.

Manholes

Deck or end diaphragm manholes inevitably leak and chloride solutions may well pond or run down inside box girder decks. Such leakage was found on the Wentbridge Viaduct in Yorkshire and on the Newhaven Swing Bridge in Sussex. In the former case, corrosion damage occurred in underlying external prestressing tendons and in the latter case severe surface corrosion arose inside the steel box.

Piers and abutment walls

Winter de-icing salt solutions can attack piers and abutment walls at the top by deck leakage rundown from the deck joints (Fig. 11.11) and at the lower levels by spash from vehicles on the roads crossed. This splash zone can extend as high as 5 m.

Any percussive tooling of the pier and abutment wall surfaces for aesthetic reasons may hasten salt-induced corrosion due to the cover cracking inflicted (Fig. 11.12). Extra reinforcement cover should be provided in accordance with clause 5.8.2 of BS 5400 part 4.

Fig. 11.11 (below). Leaking deck expansion joint

Fig. 11.12 (right). Pier corrosion, Lincoln

11.4. Proposed measures to improve salt attack durability

With recourse only to some reconsideration of traditional procedures it is possible, with very little extra effort, to reduce considerably salt attack vulnerability in the design, detailing and specification of new concrete and steel–concrete composite bridges.

In addition, several new construction materials and techniques have offered varying degrees of protection to improve the salt resistance of new, existing or repaired bridges. These should be considered in conjunction with the design, detailing and specification procedures to reduce the future salt-attack vulnerability of concrete bridges.

Descriptions of these various proposed measures follow, in the general order of design, detailing, specification and new materials.

Design for deck continuity

Bridge deck expansion joints are particularly vulnerable to salt attack, affecting not only the surrounding concrete but also the underlying piers and abutments. It therefore appears logical that deck designs should set out to minimise the number of expansion joints.

The main expansion joints occur at the ends of the deck over the abutments, with intermediate joints if multi-span decks are designed as a series of simply supported spans or, worse, with cantilever and drop-in span half-joint arrangements.

The end abutment joints may always be present, except in the case of very short built-in single span decks and box culverts. Nevertheless, longer multi-span bridges have recently been built without any deck joints at all. A whole new breed of bridges has been introduced to the American scene under the general title 'integral bridges'.[10] The bridge end movement effects are now transferred to the road approaches adjacent to the bridge, possibly causing some local pavement failure and a bump. However, this is felt to be a minor problem (and one for the road maintenance engineer!) compared with bridge joint maintenance.

The further advantages of deck continuity have been covered in earlier chapters. However, the elimination of deck joints and associated leakage and

Fig. 11.13. Deck continuity as an alternative to drop-in construction

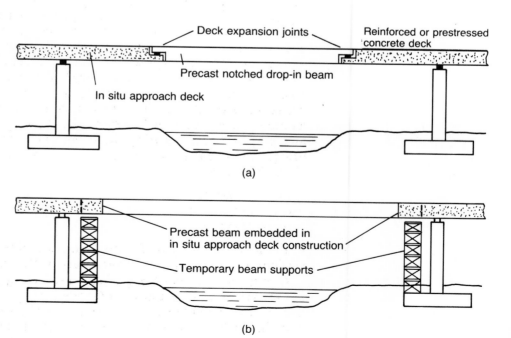

salt corrosion probably represents the greatest advantage. Figs 1.3 and 2.1, showing multi-span simply supported and continuous decks, graphically illustrate this fact.

A major new design proposal is therefore that multi-span deck continuity should be mandatory, unless soil conditions dictate otherwise, and that cantilever and drop-in spans with half-joints should never be permitted.

Fortunately, deck continuity is now commonplace and is actually encouraged by several bridge authorities. The technique of building precast beams into integral in situ crossheads was described in chapter 5 and this can be readily adapted as an alternative to cantilever and drop-in span deck arrangements (Fig. 11.13).

Design for less-vulnerable prestressing

As already stated, effective grouting of post-tensioned tendons can be difficult to execute, inspect and repair. Non-grouted lengths of tendon are not uncommon and pose a durability problem, particularly when located near the salted road surface.

Pre-tensioning does not rely on grouting and, together with the generally bigger spread of a larger number of smaller tendons, appears to be a more durable option than grouted post-tensioning tendons. Further, pre-tensioned beams generally use reinforced concrete continuity so that the tendons are in the lower half of the beam and located well away from the salt solution generating deck surfacing. The continuity reinforcement, which is close to that surfacing, can be epoxy coated to provide the required extra protection.

For continuity post-tensioned tendons located near to the deck surfacing, it is suggested that extra local deck waterproofing measures should be applied —possibly doubled-up layers of sprayed waterproofing or the judicious application of silane impregnation (see under 'New materials' in section 11.5).

In recent years it has been found that salt corrosion does not appear to be the only threat to the durability and integrity of prestressed concrete bridge decks. Investigations have indicated that prestressing tendon losses may be significantly more than the original design calculations predicted. General losses of 30–40% in 15–20 year old structures were reported in 1987. One 30 year old structure had losses as high as 66%.[11] A paper on inspection and repair of some 25-year-old Italian prestressed concrete highway bridges[12] indicated that a number of prestressed beams had sustained losses of over 60% in the tendons, requiring complete deck replacement.

The maintenance engineer is therefore faced with the knowledge that his stock of grouted post-tensioned bridge decks may be suffering not only from tendon corrosion but also from greater prestress relaxation than originally designed. With little opportunity to undertake regular inspection assessments, let alone replace corroded tendons or add new ones, it is not surprising that any proposals for ensuring more durability for new prestressed concrete bridge decks dictates the following requirements for prestressing tendons. They should be

(a) accessible
(b) inspectable
(c) replaceable

—all three operations preferably being available to the maintaining engineer without any effect on the bridge safety or the carried traffic.

A number of recent bridges have been designed to these new principles, particularly in France and West Germany (Fig. 11.14). They are box or beam and slab constructions using external prestressing tendons. In the latter case the tendons are deflected or anchored at the soffits of span crossbeam

Fig. 11.14. Externally pre-stressed flyover, France

diaphragms and the tops of pier diaphragms beneath the deck slab. Though not currently covered in BS 5400 part 4 (an omission shortly to be remedied), external prestressing has been used many times previously, offering advantages with web and flange thickness reduction.

There have also been some examples of strengthening by external prestressing, used to provide self-weight bending relief to existing reinforced concrete and steel composite decks in the UK, thereby permitting greater live loads to be carried. This is covered in chapter 12.

Widespread adoption of these ideas has not taken place because of worries about increased exposure and corrosion of the exposed tendons. To prevent such corrosion, common practice is to grease the steel cable and then coat it with a plastic sheath. In France it is sometimes preferred to weld a thick steel tube around the tendons and fill with bitumen.

There would therefore seem to be a strong case for the introduction of non-corroding prestressing tendons which could be preferably used externally to allow easy accessibility, inspectability and replaceability without interference to the carried traffic. The technology is now available in non-metallic cables of high-strength fibres (see end of section 11.5).

Design to minimise restrained early thermal shrinkage cracking

Experience has shown that in bridge structures designed to present standards, cracking can occur during construction due to the restraint of early thermal movement during the setting process in the immature concrete. This form of cracking is different from the flexural variety covered in BS 5400 and can lead to through-cracking of concrete elements which, if located in vulnerable zones, can suffer rapid salt attack. Special reinforcement design and detailing consideration is necessary, the general rule being expressed as lots of smaller diameter bars at close centres.[13]

Extra crack-minimising reinforcement is particularly required in the later stage of any staged deck construction, where restraint is usually offered by the earlier stage. Special attention must be paid to reinforced concrete parapet beam upstands poured after the deck slab, and also the webs of prestressed concrete box girders constructed in two or three stages.

The repair of salt-corroded reinforced concrete also poses problems as the newly applied patch concrete, usually not much thicker than the cover, suffers restraint from the original concrete substrate and can crack, defeating the purpose of the repair. Fig. 11.15 shows such cracking in the new concrete used to cover the repaired corrosion damage to the pier column shown in Fig. 11.12. One remedy is to use low-heat, low-shrinkage patching concrete and non-corroding mesh within the cover, or fibres, as described later.

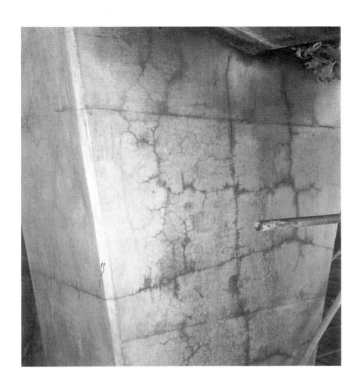

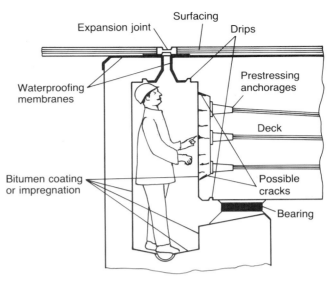

Fig. 11.15 (left). Cracked repair concrete

Fig. 11.16 (above). Expansion joint access chamber

Detailing of accessible deck end joints

Figure 11.16 shows a proposed method of treating an end abutment expansion joint to avoid some of the rundown and access problems described earlier.

The ballast wall is set back and the abutment shelf dropped as necessary to provide sufficient access way at the back of the deck for future inspections and maintenance. Short reinforced concrete corbels cantilever from the deck and the ballast wall to contain the expansion joint. The deck waterproofing is carried down the vertical and inclined edges of this joint and tucked into a drip formed under the corbel, providing rundown protection. The inclined edges allow hand access to the joint and assist in the attachment and maintenance of the membrane. It should not be too difficult to devise a joint mechanism which could be serviced or even replaced from the gallery. The remaining soffit of the corbels and the deck vertical edge are treated with a thick bitumen paint or silane impregnation to protect the prestressing anchorage recess. Similar waterproofing treatment is provided on the ballast wall, all applied from the access gallery.

Fig. 11.17. Access chamber in overbridge, Düsseldorf, Germany

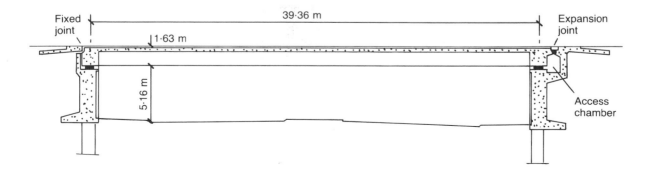

A drip is provided to the rear of the bearings to prevent any moisture migration across the deck soffit, which might occur due to failure of the drainage arrangements or excessive condensation within the access chamber.

The abutment shelf is also waterproofed with bitumen paint or silane impregnation. Adequate falls are provided to a substantial drain at the back of the abutment face.

There has not been much use of these abutment galleries in the UK, although they were proposed some time ago.[14] Currently they are recommended by the Scottish Development Department,[15] and they have been in regular use in parts of Germany for some years (Fig. 11.17).

Detailing of adequate deck drainage and drips

It is essential that all other surfaces which can suffer salt-water rundown and penetration should be waterproofed and drained to the same standard as the deck top surfaces to prevent ponding. Substantial falls should be provided where possible to reduce the build-up of deposits. Shelves and recesses where salt-laden material can accumulate should be avoided.

The interiors of box girders can be vulnerable, particularly with leak-prone manholes in the upper flanges located over prestressing cables external to the webs. All individual cells formed by webs and cross-diaphragms should be drained separately, each with individual water exits to proprietary drainage systems, or by plastic pipes through the bottom flange. The latter should protrude sufficiently from the flange to avoid soffit spread or wind splash. Waterproofing of the top surface of the bottom slab should also be considered.

Generously proportioned deck drips can prevent a lot of rundown spread and should be provided at the edges of both side cantilever slabs and the soffit of main deck slabs or box girders. The drips should end at special check features to prevent rundown and splash on underlying pier and abutment faces. Failing this, special bitumen-painted recesses should be located in the pier faces under the drips. This is particularly important on variable depth sucker or pseudo sucker decks, where soffit drips have been known to direct unsightly run-off on to supporting piers. Sometimes it is possible to inset piers and allow the drips to run harmlessly past, but bridge aesthetics generally dictate against such treatment.

Detailing of splash protection for piers and parapets

It is not difficult to design adequate protection for bridge piers and parapets subject to salt-splash corrosion. Splash tends to concentrate its attack just above the adjacent road surface, and dogs sometimes use columns as a tree substitute, promoting further attack. Fig. 11.18 shows typical treatment of a circular column pier and a parapet. The lower, vulnerable, zone of the pier is treated with a tough black bitumastic paint. To protect the bearings at the top from any salt-laden mist, which may collect or be blown back under the deck soffit, a matching black removable plastic collar is added, filled with grease if required. The overall effect can add aesthetic interest. The parapet can be treated with silane impregnation or GRP sheeting used as permanent formwork, in addition to the special concrete qualities and covers specified in Table 13 of BS 5400 part 4.

Specification of durable less-permeable concrete

Concrete durability is generally vested in the outer 50 mm or so of cover, because most long term attack comes from the surrounding environment. The three dominant external sources of deterioration, which are fairly common throughout the UK, are chlorides, carbon dioxide and sulphates. The main

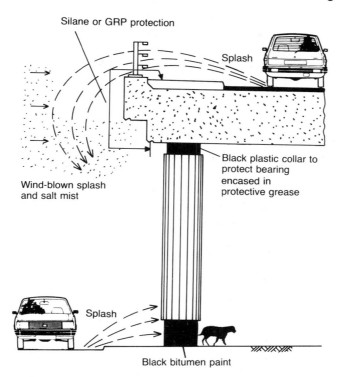

Silane or GRP protection

Splash

Wind-blown splash
and salt mist

Black plastic collar to
protect bearing
encased in
protective grease

Splash

*Fig. 11.18. Bridge edge
protection*

Black bitumen paint

internal attack comes from ASR, but this is confined to comparatively few locations, and future structures should be adequately protected by current concrete mix specification clauses.

It is thus just as important to produce a low-permeability concrete as concrete of adequate strength, particularly in the cover zone. The past few decades have seen a gradual increase in cement strengths and, as a result, mixes have required less cement to produce a desired concrete strength. With water remaining fairly constant as that amount necessary for adequate mixing and placing, this has meant an unfortunate accompanying increase in water/cement ratios.

Three main effects arise. Firstly, the concrete permeability increases as the water/cement ratio increases and the cement content decreases. Secondly, the increased water in excess of that needed for cement hydration requires an increased curing period (not always observed) which can result in a more permeable cover concrete. Thirdly, the faster-acting cement produces more heat of hydration, and restrained early thermal shrinkage can result in increased cover cracking.

It is therefore increasingly important to observe the four Cs defined by George Somerville in producing durable less-permeable concrete: constituents, curing, cover and compaction.

A fifth C, 'care', must be applied to ensure the correct application of the four. It would be very useful if this care could be monitored. It is, therefore, desirable to include regular concrete permeability testing, possibly by the ISAT method, alongside conventional strength testing.

Renewed interest is being shown in the use of ground granulated blast-furnace slag as a replacement for up to 50% of the usual Portland cement. Improved durability results from the reduced permeability and, with a lower heat of hydration, a lesser risk of cracking due to restrained early thermal shrinkage.

*Fig. 11.19. Docklands
Light Railway docks-
crossing viaduct, London*

Specification of quality assurance

It is suggested that the adoption of quality assurance procedures in design, detailing, specification and construction will eliminate at least some of the errors to which these procedures are prone. The recently completed viaduct construction for the London Docklands Light Railway was one of the first bridging projects to be subjected to QA procedures in the UK (Fig. 11.19).

As part of the QA procedures it is expected that adequate bridge maintenance manuals will be provided by the designer for the guidance of the maintaining authority.

11.5. New materials

In recent years there has been a quickening development, particularly in Germany and America, of materials which can be used for protecting concrete bridges from salt attack. Some of the impetus comes from the large sums currently being spent by the US government to tackle the country's enormous backlog of bridge maintenance. A number of these new materials appear promising and could well offer a significant range of additional protective measures for the construction of new bridges. Time must progress to demonstrate the effectiveness of such new materials. It is therefore encouraging that most of them are currently under laboratory or field investigation in the UK and, in some cases, limited use.

The materials can be classified into several groups, as described in the following sections.

Prefabricated sheet materials

Relatively inert and impermeable sheet materials can be bonded to the more vulnerable concrete surfaces to form a barrier to salt penetration. A familiar example is the bridge deck waterproofing membrane in use to considerable benefit for some four decades in the UK, and still being developed. Appearance considerations dictate that such membranes cannot be used on visible salt-vulnerable areas, such as parapets and piers in splash zones.

More visibly acceptable, neater, rigid and less susceptible than flexible deck membranes to blistering is GRC or GRP sheeting, which can be colour-matched to the surrounding concrete. These materials have been used on bridge parapets, also fulfilling the role of permanent formwork. Another recent use was sheeting bonded with epoxy compounds on to the soffits of the above-water precast concrete pilecaps of the docks-crossing viaducts of the London Docklands Light Railway (Figs 11.20 and 11.21).

Fig. 11.20. Detail of pilecap for DLR docks-crossing viaduct

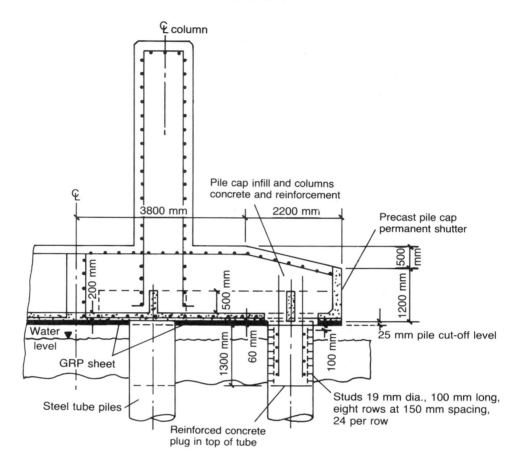

Fig. 11.21. GRP protective sheeting for pilecap

Liquid-applied surface coatings

Protective materials can be applied to the vulnerable concrete surfaces in liquid form by spray, roller or brush. They dry to form barrier coatings resistant to salt and other forms of attack. There are a number of good proprietary coatings and paints now available. Their very success in acting as an impermeable one-way barrier to the concrete can sometimes prove a weakness, as they may be susceptible to blistering and lifting from the inevitable moisture vapour seeking to get out from the concrete in the other direction as part of the long term concrete maturing process. Some materials offer a 'breathing' property to minimise this risk. Sunlight's ultra-violet action can also cause deterioration of certain exposed coatings, requiring renewal at regular intervals.

Also under this classification appear several sprayed-on bridge deck waterproofing membranes which have been used successfully recently. They are tough enough to take construction traffic prior to surfacing and, being jointless, avoid some of the 'wallpapering joint' problems of more conventional membranes (Fig. 11.22). Fig. 11.23 shows the ease of application to vertical, inclined and horizontal surfaces on a bridge treated in Yorkshire.

Fig. 11.22. Sheet waterproofing

Fig. 11.23. Sprayed waterproofing

Surface impregnation

Silane and siloxane surface impregnation are in vogue in the salt protection field. There is little doubt that, when the substances are properly applied, the concrete is impregnated to a depth of 2–4 mm with a water-repellent pore lining material which acts as a strong barrier to salt penetration. The material also allows some concrete breathing, is more or less invisible and is claimed to last longer than surface coatings. The DTp currently favours silane protection.[16]

There are also claims that the breathing ability allows some drying-out of the concrete in not overhumid climates. The associated reduction in chemical activity could mean slowing down of salt-generated reinforcement corrosion which had already started prior to impregnation.

Impregnation has been used extensively in Germany and North America. In Berlin, where severe winters require excessive road salting, it has been policy to coat all new and existing concrete bridges with silanes or siloxanes since 1967. In the early 1970s the new A4 Alpebach bridge near Cologne was used as a test bed for various types of protection against concrete freeze–thaw disintegration and salt attack. Fig. 11.24 shows adjacent test panels after 15 winters of heavy salting. The freeze–thaw pop-out damage is very evident in the panel of air-entrained concrete, but not in the silane-treated panel.

One of the first uses of silane in the UK was on the upper surface of the concrete deck of the light railway bridge shown in Fig. 11.19. In this case it was used purely as a waterproofing medium as winter de-icing salt is not used.

Below-surface protection

The inclusion of fibres of high-strength material in the concrete mix adds a crack-arresting function and toughness throughout the whole body of the structure, including, most importantly, the environment-resisting cover

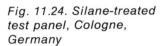

Fig. 11.24. Silane-treated test panel, Cologne, Germany

Fig. 11.25. Bridge on Manchester Metro

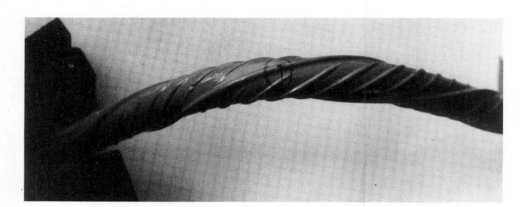

Fig. 11.26. Cracking of coating in bent epoxy-coated reinforcement

Fig. 11.27. Fluidised bed epoxy-coated reinforcement cage

concrete. Any restrained early thermal shrinkage cracking of this material will be effectively reduced, thus improving durability. Fibres of steel, stainless steel and glass, and fibrillated mesh polypropylene are currently available in the UK.

As an effective last-line defence it is now possible to obtain steel bars with a factory-applied epoxy coating. Such corrosion-resistant bars were recently used on the concrete pavement of the M18, near Doncaster, and on several bridges in Wales.[17] Fig. 11.25 shows a bridge on the Manchester Metro (completed in 1992) which incorporates epoxy-coated steel reinforcement in concrete sections of the deck. The use of this type of reinforcement is mandatory in certain areas of bridge decks for various regions of Canada and the USA.

Cutting and bending of epoxy-coated reinforcement needs care (Fig. 11.26), and straight bars should be detailed where possible. A new process of dipping completed reinforcement cages, already cut, bent and assembled, using fluidised bed technology, can avoid these possible problems (Fig. 11.27).

Non-metallic high-strength fibre prestressing tendons

Design procedures would obviously benefit by the introduction of a non-corroding prestressing system. New high-strength fibre tendons offer the required structural properties and, located under the deck, would not suffer their only major weakness, ultra-violet attack. Care would, however, be required with the location and protection of steel anchorages and deflectors, which can suffer corrosion. Also the effects of curvature, pressure and friction on the tendon at the deflectors need careful consideration. It should also be remembered that, with non-grouted tendons, if the anchorage fails the complete prestressing effect and any ultimate strength is lost, which is not the case with bonded tendons.

There are several high-strength fibre systems available based on glass or Kevlar fibres, some encased in epoxy-compound material. They can be used for pre-tensioned, post-tensioned or external prestressing applications. The

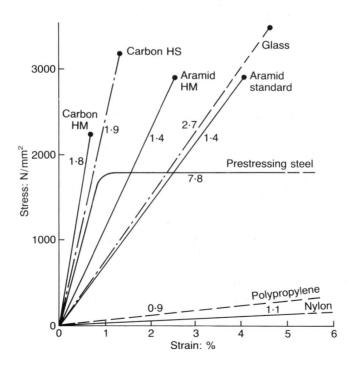

Fig. 11.28. Stress–strain curves for prestressing tendons of various materials and relative densities of materials

Fig. 11.29. High strength fibre prestressed concrete road bridge, Düsseldorf, Germany

best known systems are Polystal in Germany, Arapree in Holland and Parafi[18] in the UK. Parafi have recently developed a fire-protection sheath for their Kevlar cables, which can only be used externally. A recent TRRL report contains a useful review of the various systems available.[19] It includes a stress–strain diagram of various steel and fibre tendons, attributed to Gerritse of Arapree (Fig. 11.28).

Four prestressed concrete bridges using the Polystal system have so far been built in West Germany, and several more are planned.[20] They are all designated as 'demonstration' or 'research' projects and use Polystal bars of glass fibre embedded in epoxy. It is understood that the DTp is currently considering such a project in the UK.

The first two bridges were built in Düsseldorf—a small footbridge in 1980 and a 47 m long two-span road bridge in 1986 (Fig. 11.29). Decks were of solid concrete slab construction with embedded bonded tendons composed of 19 Polystal bars of 7·5 mm dia. in 55 mm dia. steel ducts grouted with resin-based mortar. The fourth bridge, completed in Leverkusen in 1990, also uses bonded tendons.

The third bridge was completed in West Berlin in 1989 and is a 51 m long two-span partially prestressed concrete footbridge of double T section. The Polystal tendons are unbonded and are externally located between the two webs and the underside of the deck slab. They are abutment anchored and deflected by passing under two crossbeams located in each span and over the top of the central pier crossbeam (Figs 11.30 and 11.31).

Fig. 11.30. High strength fibre externally pre-stressed concrete foot-bridge, Berlin

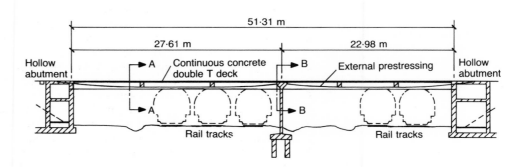

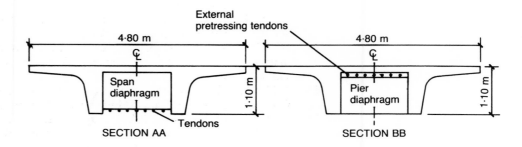

Fig. 11.31. Detail of external cables

The behaviour of the tendons in the bridges can be monitored with 2 mm thick optical-fibre sensors embedded in the middle of some of the Polystal bars.[21] All other bars are monitored using 0·5 mm dia. copper-wire sensors.

11.6. References

1. DEPARTMENT OF TRANSPORT. *Maintenance painting of highway structures. Procedure, contracting and technical requirements.* HMSO, London, 1990, DTp Advice Note BA 13/83, Part 6, Series 1900.
2. BISHOP. *Alternative to bridge painting.* Transport and Road Research Laboratory, Crowthorne, 1985, Suppl. Report 621.
3. DEPARTMENT OF TRANSPORT. *DTp specification for highway works, part 5, series 1700: structural concrete.* HMSO, London, 1986.
4. THORNS. The prediction of ice formation on roads. *J. Instn Highw. Transportn*, 1985, Aug.–Sept.
5. PULLAR-STRECKER. *Corrosion damaged concrete.* Construction Industry Research and Information Association and Butterworths, London, 1987.
6. PRICE. *Field trials on waterproofing systems for concrete bridge decks.* Transport and Road Research Laboratory, Crowthorne, Research Report 185.
7. GOHLER. Experiences with the first generation of prestressed concrete bridges in Germany. 1st Int. Conf. Bridge Management, University of Surrey, 1990.
8. JUNGWIRTH. Conserving and strengthening prestressed concrete structures. *Proc. Int. Ass. Bridge Struct. Engrs*, 1987, P-112/87.
9. WOODWARD and WILSON. Corrosion of post-tensioned tendons. *Proc. Instn Civ. Engrs*, 1991, Apr.
10. BURKE. Integral bridges. American Transportation Research Board's 69th Annual Meeting, Washington, 1990.
11. BUCHNER and LINDSELL. Testing of prestressed concrete structures during demolition. Structural Assessment Seminar, Building Research Station, Garston, 1987.
12. PETRANGELI. Inspection and repair of some highway bridges in Italy. 1st Int. Conf. Bridge Management, University of Surrey, 1990.
13. DEPARTMENT OF TRANSPORT. *Early thermal shrinkage of concrete.* HMSO, London, 1987, DTp Departmental Standard BD28/87.

14. PRITCHARD. Combatting road salt corrosion in concrete bridges—the way ahead. Symposium on Concrete Structures for the Future (International Association of Bridge and Structural Engineers), Paris, 1987.

15. HALDEN. Design and performance of weathering steel bridges on Scottish trunk roads. *Proc. Instn Civ. Engrs*, 1991, Apr.

16. DEPARTMENT OF TRANSPORT. *Criteria and material for the impregnation of concrete highway structures*. HMSO, London, 1990, DTp Departmental Standard BA33/90.

17. READ. FBECR: the fight to cure the problem. 1st Int. Conf. Bridge Management, University of Surrey, 1990.

18. BURGOYNE. Symposium on Engineering Applications of Parafil Ropes, Imperial College, London, 1988.

19. CLARKE and JACKSON. *Review of alternative materials for tension elements in bridges*. Cement and Concrete Association Services and British Cement Association, Wexham Springs, and Transport and Road Research Laboratory, Crowthorne, 1990.

20. FRANKE and WOLFF. Glass fibre tendons for prestressed concrete bridges. Congress on Challenges to Structural Engineering (International Association of Bridge and Structural Engineers), Helsinki, 1988.

21. MIESSLER and LESSING. Monitoring of load bearing structures with optical fibre sensors. Symposium on Durability of Structures (International Association of Bridge and Structural Engineers), Lisbon, 1989.

12

Bridge deck strengthening with minimum traffic disruption: *relieving and sharing load*

Fig. 12.1. Strengthened M62 Rakewood Viaduct

12.1. Introduction

An ever-expanding world demand for highways means a global stock of bridges not only increasing in numbers but also in age. At the same time, traffic and the bridge loading demands of design codes are also increasing, leading to associated expansions of bridge-strengthening programmes. The recently announced 15 year bridge rehabilitation programme described in DTp Circular Roads 2/91 is now under way in the UK. The assessments and any necessary strengthening will provide for the use of 40 t lorries and 11·5 t axle weight from 1 January 1999, as already permitted in other parts of the European Community. Costs of over £1000 million are anticipated.

Bridge strengthening inevitably requires changes to the deck structure, often accompanied by upgrading of the substructure. With associated traffic disruption costs so high, and the recently imposed lane rental charges or notional costs often exceeding the cost of the bridge strengthening (see chapter 15), a considerable amount of ingenuity has been expended by designers of late to minimise or even eliminate these costly disruptions. Fig. 12.1 shows a viaduct recently strengthened by prestressing carried out well below the heavily trafficked deck slab, requiring little, if any, interference with traffic.

This chapter initially sets out the important characteristics sought of such strengthening methods, with some discussion of methods of measuring the stress state of the existing bridge. It then describes two techniques for deck strengthening with minimum, if any, traffic disruption, by increasing deck beam bending capacity: one by relieving self-weight bending by prestressing, and the other by load-sharing with additional new steel beams.

Following on from this, chapter 13 describes the strengthening and fatigue-life extension of steel–concrete composite decks with no traffic disruption by the addition of new spring-pin shear connectors.

Chapter 14 covers the strengthening of substructures without traffic disruption by load-sharing STUs, as referred to in section 10.4.

12.2. Requirements for bridge strengthening with minimum traffic disruption

To avoid disruption to the traffic carried during the bridge strengthening operations, the following characteristics are required.

(a) Strengthening work to the deck should take place under the deck and away from the trafficked upper surface.

(b) Strengthening should be confined to adding to the existing structure, with only minor cutting or removal to acceptable safety factors.

(c) Strengthening materials should generally exclude wet construction such as in situ concreting, guniting, grouting or gluing to avoid possible separation effects due to traffic vibration during setting.

(d) Strengthening attachments to existing steel bridge decks should be fixed by bolting rather than welding because the dangers of overheating steel under service loading.

(e) Strengthening procedures involving the use of relieving loads should not overstress the existing structure during application.

The strengthening methods described in this chapter and chapters 13 and 14 are technically feasible without resort to any traffic disruption. However, some of the operations do require drilling into or applying prestress to decks subject to traffic live load. Due care will be required, preferably backed up by quality assurance procedures.

With acknowledgement to the various Murphy's laws, some engineers may consider it prudent to close the deck to traffic while drilling or prestressing is taking place. Fortunately, these are short term procedures which can be well accommodated during overnight closures.

Fig. 12.2. Bonded-plate strengthening, A23 flyover

In recent years the technique of bonding on external steel plates to concrete has offered the engineer a relatively simple, and non-intrusive, strengthening method for reinforced concrete slab bridge decks.[1] However, the epoxy-compound gluing procedure must be free from vibration, which means bridge closure and traffic disruption for several weeks. No doubt the setting times will be reduced as the technology advances, possibly reducing traffic disruption to similar overnight closures. Fig. 12.2 shows the use of the technique for the transverse strengthening of a concrete slab underbridge. Fortunately the bridge was originally constructed in two separate halves, allowing traffic on one half of the bridge while plate bonding is applied to the other, closed, half.

12.3. In situ stress measurement

When dealing with a bridge strengthening, the engineer will require to know the current state of loading and stress in the existing bridge.

Resort to the original calculations, unfortunately not always readily available, will provide the engineer with the load and stress patterns predicted by the early design. However, some of the patterns depend on behaviour assumptions which may not have been realised or may have been exceeded in practice, particularly in relation to such items as deck settlement and prestressing losses. Certainly there is growing evidence of considerable underestimation of the latter phenomenon in early prestressed bridges.[2,3]

Live loading and temperature loading effects on deck and substructure can be readily measured by reading the difference between the unloaded and loaded condition of suitably installed strain gauging. However, the self-weight, settlement and prestress loss effects cannot be measured using this same strain equipment, because the initial unloaded state was never gauged. In addition, unknown creep strains in older concrete structures would generally be greater than elastic strains, making long term readings unreliable even if gauges had been installed at the time of bridge construction.

These self-weight, settlement and prestress loss effects are generally termed

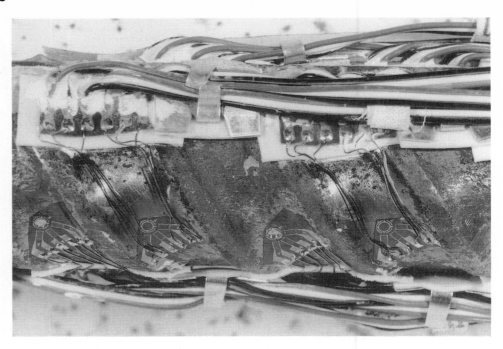

Fig. 12.3. In situ stress gauges on reinforcing bar

in situ stresses. The engineer who wishes to know the total loads and stresses in his existing structure therefore has the problem of measuring these in situ stresses. In effect, this means measuring the loads and stresses in the existing structure in its early morning state, with no traffic loading and minimum, if any, differential temperature loading.

Fortunately, several methods have been developed in recent years for measuring in situ stresses in steel or concrete.[4] Most rely on using special small electrical strain gauges arranged in multi-vector rosettes to measure strain changes around small holes or cores as they are cut into steel or concrete. The strain changes around the disturbed material can be used to establish the in situ tensile or compressive stresses in the material. Another method uses jacks installed in a slot cut in the concrete surface to restore the strain relaxations caused by the slot-cutting in adjacent strain gauges. The jack pressure is then a direct measure of the in situ concrete load in the slot area, and hence the in situ stress.

One long-established technique used in mechanical engineering, known as the 'blind hole drilling method' of residual stress determination, has been developed for bridge engineering to measure in situ stresses in steel reinforcement and individual wires of prestressing strands.

The procedure for steel reinforcement is to remove a small amount of the concrete cover and bond a very small three-element vectored strain gauge rosette to the bar surface midway between bar ribs (Fig. 12.3). A high-speed dental-type air turbine drill is used to form a 1·6 mm dia. hole at the intersection of the three vectored strain gauges to a depth of 1·6 mm, drilled in twelve increments.

The change in strain is measured after each hole increment is drilled, and used to plot the variation of relieved strain with depth. The relationship between this rate of change of strain and the desired residual strain is complex,[5] not least because of the locked-in residual strains in the bar due to the rolling process during manufacture. The basic principle can perhaps be explained by imagining a hole drilled in a piece of strip elastic. As the elastic is stretched, the circular hole becomes oval in the direction of the tension, the ovality being a measure of the intensity of this tension.

Proving tests indicate that in situ tensile and compressive stress measurements in concrete or steel can be relied on to accuracies as high as $\pm 5\%$. This adds a powerful tool for the engineer seeking to determine a more accurate load and stress pattern in his existing bridge before attempting to strengthen it. Of course, the techniques can prove equally valuable in the modification of bridges described in chapter 15.

Various techniques have been used with success recently to establish in situ stresses in reinforcement on an M1 overbridge, in prestressing strands on an M62 railway bridge and in concrete on the M2 Medway bridge.

12.4. Self-weight relief strengthening by prestressing

Conventional prestressing of a bridge deck imposes a permanent direct compression together with a bending moment which counters, or relieves, the applied dead load moments. The bending moment reduction effect of added prestressing can also be used to advantage in relieving dead load bending in existing overloaded decks of reinforced concrete, steel or composite steel–concrete deck structures. This dead load bending relief can be sufficient to reduce the deck bending under full dead and live loading to permissible limits. Alternatively, a bridge deck can be upgraded to carry increased superimposed dead or live loading, or both, equivalent to the dead load bending relief imposed.

In general, the direct compression effect of the added prestressing is not helpful. Reinforced concrete allowable compressive stresses are usually lower than with prestressed concrete, and extra compression in steel structures can lead to plate stability problems. It is therefore beneficial to mobilise as much of the prestressing bending moment reduction as possible, and there is every advantage in locating the prestressing tendons at the beam extremities or even beyond.

Sections 12.5 and 12.6 describe applications of this technique to a reinforced concrete deck and to simply supported and continuous multi-span composite concrete/steel girder decks. Strangely, the technique is not readily

Fig. 12.4. Rail spans of the River Tawe crossing, Carmarthen

Fig. 12.5 (above left). Arch within an arch, River Tawe crossing

Fig. 12.6 (above right). Deflector plate fixing

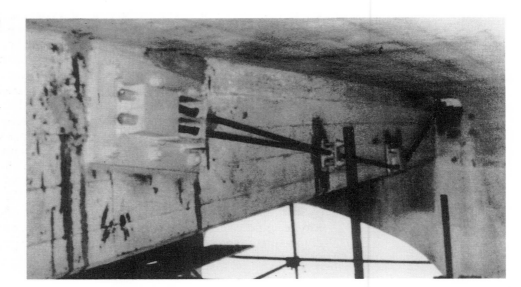

Fig. 12.7. Prestressing cable deflection

Fig. 12.8. Strengthening completed

applicable to the strengthening of prestressed concrete decks. However, it can be used to top up prestress loss due to excessive creep.[3]

12.5. Strengthening a reinforced concrete bridge deck by prestressing

A major trunk road crossing of the River Tawe was built in Carmarthen in 1938. The river was spanned by three reinforced concrete arches and the road and rail tracks running along the river banks were crossed by a series of reinforced concrete beam and slab approach spans (Fig. 12.4).

By 1978 it became necessary to strengthen the whole crossing to cater for the increased traffic and newer bridge code requirements. The nature of the crossing required minimum, if any, traffic disruption. Several innovative techniques were developed,[6] including the building of new reinforced concrete arches using the existing arches as falsework (Fig. 12.5), and the use of steel beams to strengthen some of the original beam and slab approach decks, described in section 12.7.

Self-weight relief strengthening was applied to a three-span section of the approach viaducts. The continuous 8 m beam and slab spans crossed the riverbank road and railway and the strengthening method adopted required no disruption to either the traffic carried or crossed.

Deck strengthening was carried out under the deck by external prestressing to reduce self-weight bending sufficiently to allow the imposition of extra live loading without increasing overall deck bending.

The prestressing anchor and deflector plates were fixed to the opposite sides of each beam by clamping on to epoxy mortar bedding using HSFG bolts drilled through the beams (Fig. 12.6). The bolts were also grouted with an epoxy mortar to ensure that the prestressing force was transmitted from the anchorages to the beam by the twin actions of end bearing of the bolts and friction and adhesion generated by the combined HSFG action and epoxy bedding.

The prestressing cables were 0·6 in (15 mm) dia. Dyform strands encased in protective plastic sheathing (Figs 12.7 and 12.8). No further protection was provided for these external tendons, though provision was made for future topping-up of the tendon load if found necessary.

Fig. 12.9. Strengthening simply supported girders, USA

Fig. 12.10. Original M62 Rakewood Viaduct

12.6. Strengthening a steel–concrete composite bridge deck by prestressing

In the late 1980s successful experimental work on models and existing structures of simply supported composite steel girder/concrete deck slab construction strengthened by prestressing had been undertaken at Iowa State University, USA.[7] The prestressing bars were located on top of the girder bottom flanges and stressed via bolted-on anchors (Fig. 12.9).

The opportunity to apply this strengthening technique in the UK, extended to a continuous bridge deck, arose in 1987.[8] Rakewood Viaduct, located adjacent to the Lancashire/Yorkshire boundary, carries the dual three-lane M62 across a 36 m deep valley (Fig. 12.10). The 34·4 m wide viaduct was constructed between 1967 and 1969 and is a six-span continuous structure with two end spans of 36·6 m and four main spans of 45·7 m, giving an overall length of 256 m. Construction is of braced continuous steel plate girders 3·05 m deep, composite with an in situ reinforced concrete deck slab.

The steep M62 gradients coupled with the high percentage of commercial vehicles using the motorway resulted in severe congestion of the two near-side lanes by heavy vehicles, with cars effectively restricted to the off-side lane. Additionally, the site is very exposed, and can suffer high winds and, in winter, severe snow and icing. To alleviate some of these problems it was decided that a climbing lane and a new hard shoulder should be provided for this section of the eastbound carriageway.

Rakewood Viaduct lies within this climbing section and, to avoid extensive viaduct widening, it was further decided that the present hard shoulder across the viaduct should be used as the fourth eastbound running lane, the new hard shoulder being discontinued for this short length.

Inspections and assessments undertaken in 1986 and 1987 indicated that the viaduct had stood up well to the rigorous environment and required only minor salt corrosion repair treatment. However, the bridge, originally designed to BS 153, was assessed to the current BS 5400 bridge code. The increased live loading associated with BS 5400, together with the road layout change from three lanes plus hard shoulder to four lanes, meant heavier design loading on the structure. The main shortfall was identified as an approximate 40% overloading in the steel girder compression flanges over the piers.

The overstressing of the bottom flanges over the piers by the proposed upgrading was complicated by the fact that the BS 5400 assessment also showed that the flanges were almost at allowable stress level under deck self-weight alone.

A previous example of a similar strengthening requirement for two other bridges over the M62 was examined. The bridges had been assessed in the troubled Merrison days of 1972 and found to be overstressed under self-weight alone.[9] The strengthening procedure required reversal of most of the self-weight bending by jacking from temporary trestles located in the motorway (Figs 12.11 and 12.12). Extra steel plates were added to the box

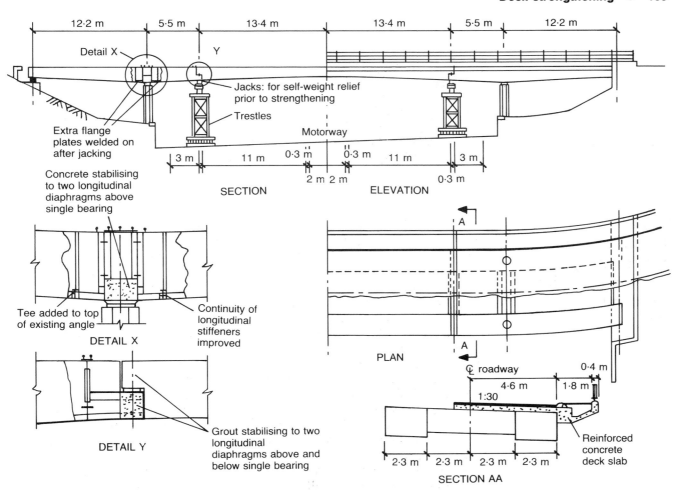

SECTION

ELEVATION

12.2 m | 5.5 m | 13.4 m | 13.4 m | 5.5 m | 12.2 m

Detail X

Y

Jacks: for self-weight relief prior to strengthening

Trestles

Motorway

Extra flange plates welded on after jacking

3 m | 11 m | 0.3 m | 0.3 m | 11 m | 3 m

2 m 2 m

0.3 m

Concrete stabilising to two longitudinal diaphragms above single bearing

Tee added to top of existing angle

Continuity of longitudinal stiffeners improved

DETAIL X

DETAIL Y

Grout stabilising to two longitudinal diaphragms above and below single bearing

PLAN

A

A

℄ roadway

0.4 m

4.6 m | 1.8 m

1:30

Reinforced concrete deck slab

2.3 m | 2.3 m | 2.3 m | 2.3 m

SECTION AA

Fig. 12.11 (above). Jacking out self-weight on early M62 bridge

Fig. 12.12 (right). Jacking under way

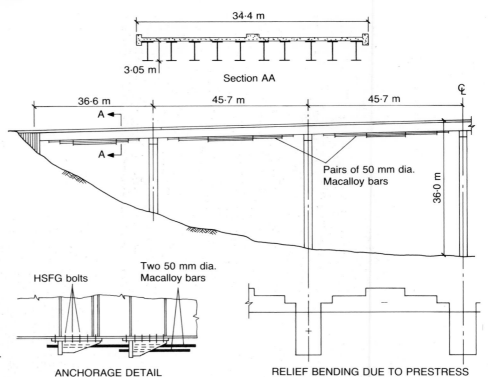

34·4 m

Section AA

3·05 m

36·6 m   45·7 m   45·7 m

Pairs of 50 mm dia.
Macalloy bars

36·0 m

Two 50 mm dia.
Macalloy bars

HSFG bolts

*Fig. 12.13. Rakewood
Viaduct strengthening procedure*

ANCHORAGE DETAIL

RELIEF BENDING DUE TO PRESTRESS

girder bottom flanges by difficult overhead welding before the jacks were
released and the self-weight was released on to the strengthened girders.

A similar proposal to add extra flange metal at Rakewood would have
required a considerable degree of temporary unloading of the structure prior
to the addition of the extra steel, and then reloading. Such unloading would
have required jacking off the valley floor or staged jacking and release operations off the pier tops. Both would have been complex and highly expensive
operations, as traffic on the viaduct was required to be virtually uninterrupted
at all times.

In the circumstances, it was decided to adopt permanent 'unloading' by
prestressing rather than strengthening by the addition of flange plates at the
pier sections.

Figure 12.13 indicates the procedure, which first requires the attachment of
fabricated steel anchors to the underside of each steel beam bottom flange by
HSFG bolting. Three pairs of 50 mm or 36 mm dia. Macalloy prestressing
bars of overlapping lengths are then attached under each flange between piers.
Upon stressing, hogging bending is set up in the midspan regions of the beam.
However, it is the parasitic sagging moment over the piers, caused by deck
continuity, which performs the required 'unloading' to acceptable stress limits
in the bottom girder flanges over the piers.

The dispersion of the high anchorage loads (Figs 12.14 and 12.15) into the
girder flanges and webs, and the associated local web-stiffener design had been
examined using three-dimensional finite element techniques (Fig. 12.16).
Special consideration was also given to the provision of node supports to
prevent wind vibration of the stressing bars and, of course, anti-corrosion
protection.

The prestressing of the girders proceeded in 1989 with minimum disruption
of the M62 traffic. The downstanding overlapped Macalloy bars and anchorages (Fig. 12.17) caused little visual intrusion to the deck (Fig. 12.1).

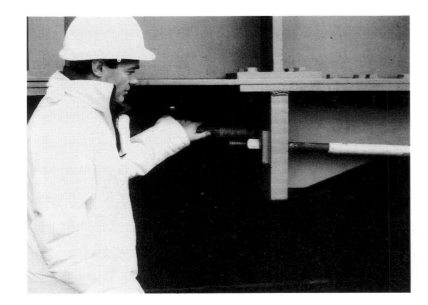

Fig. 12.14 (left). Prestressing tendon anchor

Fig. 12.15 (below). Prestressing tendons under bottom flange

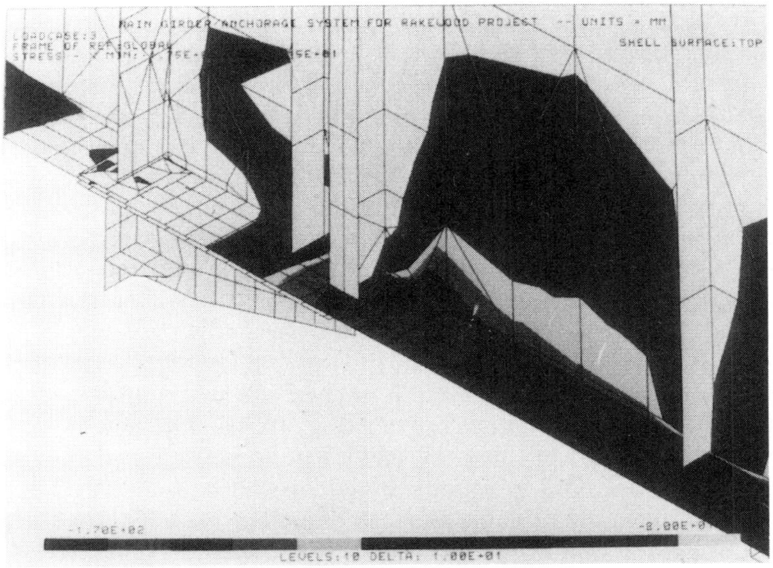

Fig. 12.16 (above). Three-dimensional finite element analysis, end anchorage zone

Fig. 12.17 (right). Overlapping anchorages

Fig. 12.18. Grouting grout bags

Fig. 12.19. Grout bags used for M5/M6 Midlands Links repair

12.7. Strengthening a reinforced concrete bridge deck by load-sharing with new steel beams

In common with the earlier American work, it was found that the strengthening prestressing loads could be reduced by excessive substructure restraint. It is therefore essential to ensure that the deck-support bearings can articulate freely in response to the newly imposed movements due to deck prestressing.

It is believed that the technique could be improved further by substituting high strength fibre composite prestressing tendons, as described in chapter 11, for the steel Macalloy bars. Not only would the tendons require no corrosion-protection, but also their fatigue properties would be better, in part because the lower elastic modulus means that the range of tensions induced by live load on the deck would be less.

A reinforced concrete bridge deck can be strengthened by the use of new steel beams placed directly between or under the existing beams. The new beams may be supported off the existing piers or off newly constructed piers and foundations. The design analysis is usually based on the new and existing beams acting together, although not compositely, along their full lengths such that applied loading is shared in proportion to their stiffnesses. Nevertheless, it is now possible to build in beneficial composite action by using the new spring-pin shear connectors described in chapter 13. The innovatory technique developed related to the establishment of the structural filling of the small and generally variable gap between the new and the in-service beams.

The method was initially used on several spans of the reinforced concrete beam deck described in section 12.5. It had to take account of the fact that the gap depth varied between 30 mm and 75 mm because of the undulating nature of the existing beam soffit. There was also lack of accessibility, with the narrow gap extending over the 250 mm width of the new steel beam flange.

The solution was to use circular nylon-reinforced grout bags, with circumferences ranging between 700 mm and 500 mm, initially laid flat over the steel beam top flange. The bags were then pressure-filled with sand–cement grout to take up the varying gaps and left to harden (Fig. 12.18). The pressurised grout was not only contained but unaffected by any vibrations arising from traffic during setting. A recent application on the M5/M6 Midlands Links repair contracts is shown in Fig. 12.19. The grout bag is used to establish load contact across the variable gap between the deck slab and the steel beam.

Fig. 12.20. Arch strengthening

The variable gap problem also occurs when existing arches are strengthened by the incorporation of suitably bent steel beams (Fig. 12.20). Gap filling and load transfer can be readily established with grout bags without interfering with traffic.

12.8. References

1. DEPARTMENT OF TRANSPORT. *Strengthening of concrete highway structures using externally bonded plates.* DTp, London, 1989, draft advice note BA 30/89.
2. BUCHNER and LINDSELL. Testing of prestressed concrete structures during demolition. Structural Assessment Seminar, Building Research Station, Garston, 1987.
3. PETRANGELI. Inspection and repair of some highway bridges in Italy. 1st Int. Conf. Bridge Management, University of Surrey, 1990.
4. PRITCHARD. Measuring in situ stresses in damaged reinforced concrete beams. Structural Faults and Repair Conference, London, 1987.
5. OWENS. Calibration of the centre hole technique of residual stress measurement. Proceedings BSSM Conference, Aston University, Birmingham, 1980.
6. HARRIS. Bridge within a bridge. *Concrete Mag.*, 1980, Jan.
7. KLAIBER *et al.* Strengthening of single span steel beam bridges by post-tensioning. Structural Faults 85, 2nd Int. Conf. Structural Faults and Repair, London, 1985.
8. PRITCHARD. Strengthening of the M62 Rakewood Viaduct. Construction Marketing Symposium on Strengthening and Repair of Bridges, Leamington Spa, 1988.
9. PRITCHARD and SPOONER. The impact of Merrison and some related steel box girder analysis and design applied to bridge strengthening. Australian Institute of Structural Engineers Conference on Steel Development, Newcastle, Australia, 1973.

Extending the fatigue life of steel–concrete composite decks without traffic disruption: *spring-pin shear connectors*

Fig. 13.1. Spring-pin shear connectors

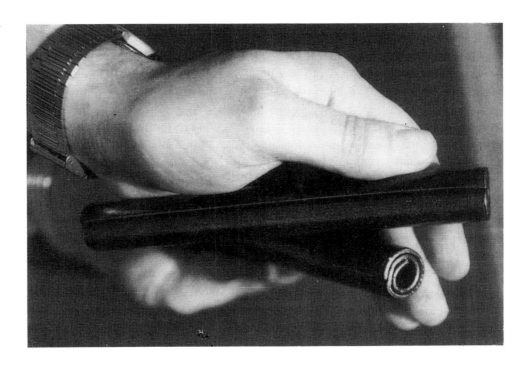

13.1. Introduction

This chapter describes the introduction of a new type of spring-pin shear connector (Fig. 13.1) for strengthening and extending the fatigue life of existing bridge decks constructed of steel girders supporting and composite with reinforced concrete deck slabs. The pin development occurred as a result of the recently required upgrading of the viaducts carrying London's Docklands Light Railway (DLR). This is described, together with the tests on the new shear connector carried out by the Welding Institute. After further describing the installation of the connectors, which required no interference to the existing train services, the chapter concludes with some recommendations for further development of the new technique.

13.2. Docklands Light Railway upgrading

The rapidly developing London Docklands lie just east of the highly congested financial area of the City of London. An interconnecting new light rail service for the further development of both regions was completed in 1987. The 12·1 km system, linking Tower Hill in the City with the Isle of Dogs and Stratford in Docklands included 2 km of new steel composite decks[1,2] (Fig. 13.2).

Even before the 1987 opening a decision had been made to locate a massive new building complex, Canary Wharf, to straddle one of the DLR stations. With a projected eightfold increase in passenger traffic, it was necessary to provide doubled trains and increased trip frequencies when the complex (Fig. 13.3) was part-completed in 1991.

The projected increase in train loads and frequencies reduced the originally designed fatigue life of the viaduct decks and this represented a major upgrading requirement,[3] leading to the development of the new shear connectors.

Fig. 13.2. Original docks-crossing viaduct

*Fig. 13.3 (above). Canary
Wharf strengthened docks-
crossing viaduct carrying
doubled-up train*

*Fig. 13.4 (right). Cross-
section of original DLR
viaducts*

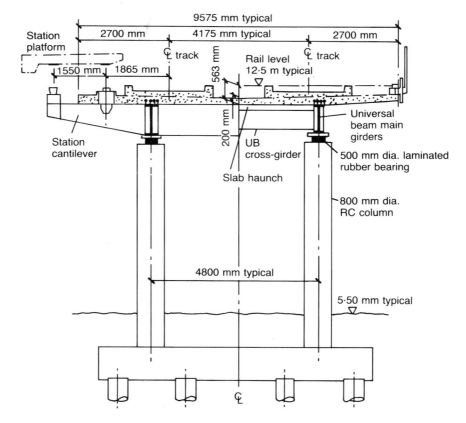

Fig. 13.5. Stud shear connectors on original DLR viaducts

The original viaduct decks are generally of continuous composite construction, with an in situ reinforced concrete deck slab supported by and composite with twin steel universal or plate girders (Fig. 13.4).

The associated design of the decks to BS 5400 established that fatigue considerations were a critical factor, particularly in the 19 mm dia. welded-stud shear connectors (Fig. 13.5). As a result of the increase in weight and frequency of trains after 1991, the fatigue life would suffer considerable reduction, in some cases as much as 75%. Strengthening measures were required to restore the fatigue life to the original design of 120 years. Additional shear connectors installed between the original 19 mm welded-stud connectors would relieve the loads on these connectors sufficiently to accomplish this.

Technically the easiest solution was to drill out holes through the deck slabs from above and install new 19 mm stud connectors, in clusters of three or four to optimise the hole size and economies of installation. Practically, this would have been extremely disruptive and costly to undertake with a live train service operation.

The upwards installation of new shear connectors through the top flange of the steel girders was also examined. Several types of connector were considered, including 20 mm dia. spring steel tension-pin fasteners. These offered the advantage of a readily achieved force fit into a hole drilled up through the steel flange and lower section of the concrete deck slab with no requirement for traffic-sensitive grouting, gluing, welding or traffic disruption.

Tension pins are now a universally accepted fastener with applications throughout all types of industry. They are compressible hollow-spring steel tubular pins with a chamfered driving nose. A force fit is obtained by jacking or hammer-driving the pin into a drilled hole with a slightly smaller diameter. There are two types, one a Spirol pin which relies on a force fit by the tightening during driving of its $2\frac{1}{4}$-turn spiral coil, and the other a cylindrical pin with a longitudinal slot which closes on driving (Fig. 13.6).

The benefit of causing no interference to the train service had to be balanced against the unknown shear and fatigue parameters of the pins used as composite deck shear connectors. Strength and fatigue testing on push-out samples was therefore initiated by the strengthening contractor.

13.3. Testing the new shear connectors

The objectives of the testing programme were to investigate the strength, stiffness, and fatigue characteristics of spring-pin fasteners, and compare them with the existing stud shear connectors. Strength and fatigue properties were required to be at least equal to those of the studs, and a stiffness equivalent to at least 50% of a stud at working load was required as a desirable minimum.

The number of spring-pin fasteners required as additional shear connectors for the composite beam decks was a function of the fastener stiffness. Thus, the stiffer the spring-pin fastener the less drilling and pin insertion would be required on site, with obvious economic benefits. This gave a strong incentive during testing to produce the stiffest fastener.

The static and cyclic tests were carried out at the Welding Institute in Cambridge in 1987 and 1988.[4] The test push-out specimen recommended in Fig. 2 of BS 5400 part 5 was not suitable as it was impossible to drill and drive the pins from the underside of the flanges of the small universal beam used in the test.

Twelve specimens with the concrete slab cast between two steel cheek plates coated with a bond-breaking compound were therefore fabricated (Fig. 13.7). When the concrete had reached the specified strength of $40 \, N/mm^2$ the holes were drilled and the pins driven—simulating the conditions which would exist on site. To save time and bit wear the holes were drilled to within 2 mm of full thickness with a conventional bit, and the remaining length plus the hole in the concrete with a diamond bit. Fig. 13.6 shows some of the pins tested in comparison with the original 19 mm stud connectors.

Fig. 13.6. Slotted and spiral pins (cross-sections shown at double the scale of longitudinal sections): (a) standard 19 mm welded stud; (b) 20 mm heavy-duty slotted tension pin; (c) 20 mm heavy-duty Spirol tension pin

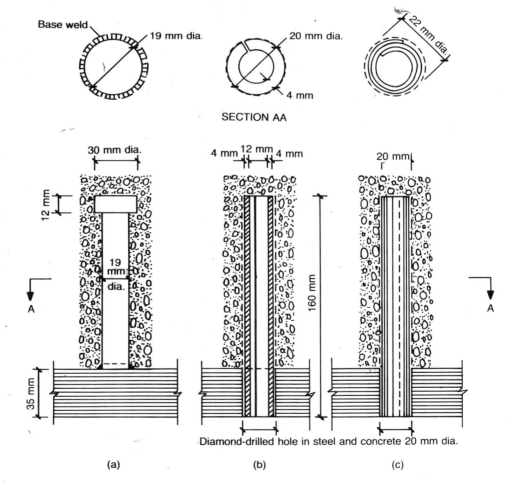

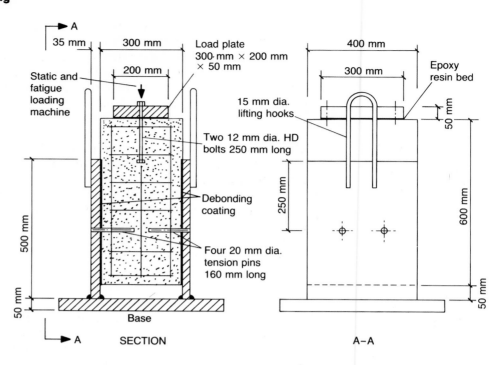

Fig. 13.7. Testing specimens

The standard 125 mm long 19 mm dia. shear connectors are as specified in Table 7 of BS 5400 part 5. They are manufactured from high-tensile steel with a specified yield of 385 N/mm². Shear is mainly transmitted through the base weld, and pull-out is resisted by the 30 mm dia. 12 mm thick head. Single shear strength is 139 kN.

The slotted tension pins tested were heavy-duty pins 20 mm dia. and 160 mm long. They are manufactured from 4 mm thick special spring steel, 55 Si 7, DIN 17222, with a 1400–1800 N/mm² tensile strength. The ultimate strength in single shear is 140 kN. The pins have a diameter of 20·5–20·9 mm before insertion into a drilled hole with a recommended diameter of 20·0–20·3 mm. The Spirol spring pins tested were heavy-duty pins 20 mm dia. and 160 mm long. They are manufactured from 2·2 mm thick special spring AISI 615OH alloy steel, with a Rockwell C hardness reading of 43–52, and are spirally wound to form $2\frac{1}{4}$ turns. The ultimate strength in single shear is 170 kN. The pins have a diameter of 20·4–21·0 mm before insertion into a drilled hole with a recommended diameter of 19·85–20·25 mm.

The force fit compresses the slotted pin or the spiral coil and provides a good interface shear connection, with a large pull-out resistance afforded by the spring-loaded friction between the pin and the hole face. However, sufficient pull-out resistance was already available in the DLR deck from the original adjacent shear stud heads.

The tests indicated that both types of 20 mm dia. tension-pin shear connector had superior strength and fatigue properties to the original 19 mm welded studs. The pin stiffnesses at anticipated service loading were slightly less than for the original studs at first service loading, but equal or greater on subsequent loading after initial set had been induced. Under cyclic loading, permanent set increased, but to a much smaller extent that that predicted for the original shear studs under a similar loading regime. Thus, on insertion, tension pins will be slightly less stiff than the adjacent original stud connectors due to initial set. However, with increasing live load applications, the fatigue set increases more on the studs than on the pin connectors. As a result the relative stiffness of the pins will increase beyond that of the studs. This reversed relative stiffness will of course cause some shear load shedding to the stronger pin connectors.

The superior fatigue properties of the tension pins came from the fact that attachment to the steel girder was by a force fit rather than a weld. The 20 mm tension pins were therefore conservatively designed as equivalent in strength and stiffness to the original 19 mm stud connectors.

13.4. Installation of the new shear connectors

The spiral Spirol-type spring pins had slightly better properties as shear connectors than the slotted pins and were chosen for installation by the contractor. Close tolerance holes were diamond-drilled between the existing welded-stud connectors, and cadmium-plated Spirol pins were jacked into place with the assistance of a special lubricant (Fig. 13.8). All operations were undertaken without interfering with the frequent train service (Fig. 13.9). The pins were inset 2 mm into the steel flange and the holes filled with an approved sealant prior to local repainting.

13.5. Further development

In a wider context, the new Spirol spring-pin connector may well offer a simple method of strengthening or extending the fatigue life of some of the large world stock of existing steel–concrete composite bridge decks. These may require upgrading due to increasing traffic loading and intensity or in order to conform to codes to which they were not originally designed. A large component of the cost of any such strengthening lies in the level of traffic disruption. The new connector is installed from under the deck and is a dry fixing not requiring operations sensitive to traffic vibration such as grouting, welding or gluing. The non-interference with traffic and the absence of disruption costs is obviously an important additional benefit.

The Spirol connector is a well-proven fastening device in industry and there appears to be no reason why it cannot be used with confidence in this new

Fig. 13.8. Jacking Spirol pins into place

Fig. 13.9. Pin installation on trafficked viaduct

bridging application. The Spirol connector itself is an inexpensive quality-controlled product. It requires close tolerance, constant diameter holes drilled through into the steel flange and concrete deck slab, and these can prove more expensive than the connectors, particularly using diamond drilling. Undoubtedly, further development will reduce these drilling costs.

The superior fatigue properties of the connector itself might well be usefully developed for new composite bridge decks subjected to severe fatigue conditions.

13.6. References

1. HAYWARD and PRITCHARD. London Docklands Light Railway new viaducts. Proc. Canadian Society for Civil Engineering 2nd Int. Conf. Short or Medium Span Bridges, Ottawa, 1986.
2. RICHMOND and CHURCHMAN. Docklands Light Railway: engineering studies and tender design of bridge and viaduct structures. *J. Instn Struct. Engrs*, 1986, Nov.
3. PILGRIM and PRITCHARD. Docklands Light Railway and subsequent upgrading, design and construction of bridges and viaducts. *Proc. Instn Civ. Engrs*, 1990, Aug.
4. *Welding Institute Bulletin*, Cambridge, 1988, May–June.

14

Strengthening bridge substructures with minimum traffic disruption: *adding shock transmission units to existing bridges for horizontal load sharing*

Fig. 14.1. Shock transmission units on the London Docklands Light Railway

14.1. Introduction

The Department of Transport's programme for assessment and strengthening of highway bridges and structures, referred to in section 12.1, will considerably add to the number of existing simply supported multi-span viaducts requiring substructure strengthening.

Some of the integrity assessments will indicate that the supporting piers are understrength due to increases in the traction and braking loading since the original design, possibly accompanied by structural integrity damage generated by road salt, carbonation or alkali–silica reaction.

In general, any repairs and strengthening procedures are less disruptive to carried road traffic than deck repair and strengthening because the work takes place under the deck. Nevertheless, any cutting-away and subsequent strengthening of the piers will prudently require some disruption to the carried traffic. It is also possible that such operations will disrupt heavily trafficked roads, railways or waterways crossed by the bridge.

With the costs of disruption so high, every effort should be made by the bridge designer to strengthen the piers with little or no disruption.

The STUs described in chapter 10 offer such possibilities to the designer, and the following sections, 14.2 and 14.3, demonstrate how substructure strengthening can be achieved by load-sharing among the piers of a viaduct or between adjacent viaducts.[1]

14.2. STUs for load-sharing between piers

A number of viaducts requiring strengthening feature long sequences of simply supported deck spans, often carried on a series of high substructure piers. This is particularly evident at major river crossings, where high navigation clearances require long approach viaducts (Fig. 14.2).

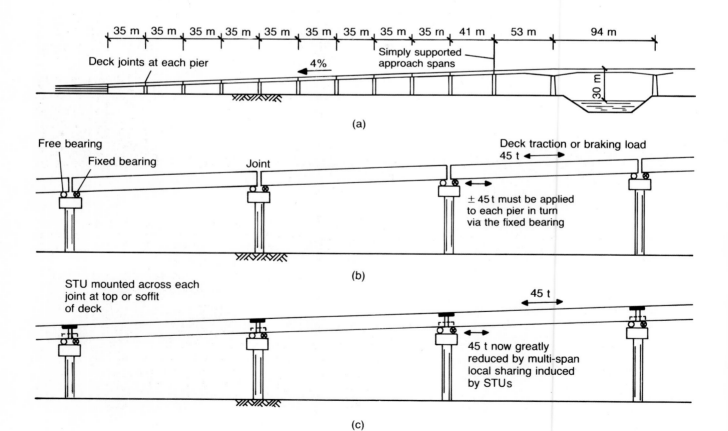

The piers under each simply supported span carry fixed bearings for one span alongside free bearings for the adjacent span, as indicated in section 10.3. As also indicated, the design longitudinal traction and braking forces must be individually applied to each deck span throughout the viaduct, with resistance offered by the pier carrying the fixed bearings of that particular span.

By connecting STUs to the deck ends supported by the free bearings and to the top of the bearing shelf, as shown in Fig. 14.2, temporary deck fixity can be gained during traction and braking. As with the new multi-span simply supported deck using STUs described in section 10.3, load-sharing will occur between all the piers, and possibly abutments, during traction and braking. The load-sharing will depend on the stiffnesses of individual piers and possibly abutments, but will inevitably considerably reduce the individual traction and braking forces applied to each pier.

This reduction in shear and bending on each pier and its foundations may mean that any increased traction and braking loading requirement can be

Fig. 14.2 (facing page). Pier horizontal load sharing for existing simply supported viaducts using STUs: (a) typical navigable river or canal crossing; (b) enlarged detail of approach span; (c) approach spans with STUs

Fig. 14.3. STUs as part of the M5/M6 Midlands Links crosshead replacement, Birmingham

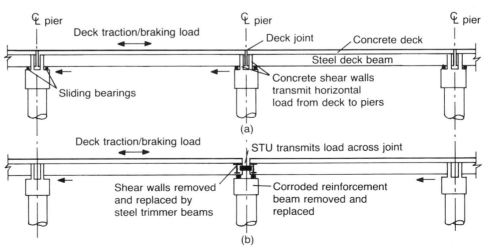

Fig. 14.4. Transmission of traction and braking force via STUs: (a) bridge before repair; (b) bridge after repair

Fig. 14.5. Seven-span DLR viaduct

Fig. 14.6. Horizontal load sharing between DLR viaducts; (a) method of linking separate viaducts in order to distribute increased longitudinal forces; (b) detail of shock transmission unit and mounting

absorbed without any need for pier or foundation strengthening. Alternatively, it may mean that environmentally damaged piers can be safely loaded by the sharing-out of the originally designed traction and braking loading.

Of course, the STUs can be attached with no traffic disruption and, indeed, they offer strengthening economy over usual pier strengthening procedures, besides the considerable savings in this freedom from traffic disruption.

Figures 14.3 and 14.4 show STUs used recently in a complex replacement of a salt-corroded reinforced concrete crosshead supporting a section of the heavily trafficked deck of the M5/M6 Midland Links viaducts in Birmingham. The removal of the corroded crosshead included twin shear walls which served

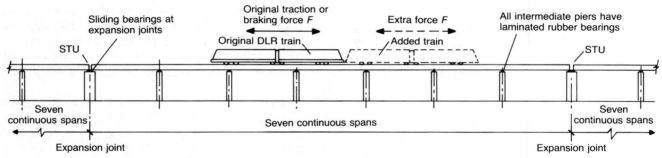

Extra traction and braking force shared with adjacent seven span viaducts
via STUs at expansion joints

(a)

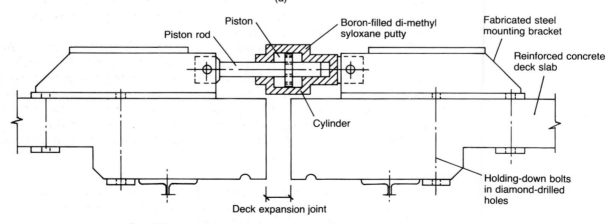

One STU is mounted on viaduct centre line between the two tracks

(b)

Fig. 14.7. DLR STU installed

not only to support the deck edges either side of the deck expansion joint but also to transmit deck traction and braking loads down to the crosshead and pier. The new steel trimmer beams visible took over the slab edge support duty, while traction and braking loads were transmitted through the strut-tie STU links fixed to the decks either side of the expansion joint on to the shear walls and supporting piers either side of the crosshead replacement pier (Fig. 14.4).

14.3. STUs for load-sharing between viaducts

The breathtaking development of London's Canary Wharf and the requirement to increase the originally planned capacity of the Docklands Light Railway (DLR) eightfold has been described in section 13.2. The capacity increase is partially effected by doubling up the existing two-car trains.

The trains are automatic, and braking and traction commands are computer-controlled. The horizontal forces generated are resisted by the piers forming the substructure.

A typical viaduct is continuous over seven spans between deck expansion joints. Train traction and braking horizontal loading, together with any wind loading, is shared among the slender reinforced concrete piers, which generally support the deck by means of rubber bearings (Figs 14.5 and 13.4).

Doubling the length of the trains during 1991 meant considerable increases in the horizontal loads arising from the traction and braking effects. The existing substructures were not designed for this increased loading, and original proposals involved extensive strengthening of bearings, piers and foundations—a costly and disruptive procedure.

The load-sharing idea was adapted for the DLR substructure strengthening and the simple introduction of STUs at the deck joints (Figs 14.6, 14.7 and 14.1) avoided the costly and disruptive strengthening procedures. Some of the increased traction and braking effects of a particular seven-span viaduct are transmitted by impact through the STUs into the adjacent viaducts. The load-sharing is sufficient to keep the horizontal loading on the bearings, piers and foundations of such multi-span viaducts within the original design limits.

14.4. Reference

1.   PRITCHARD. Shock transmission units for bridge strengthening. Congress on Challenges to Structural Engineering (International Association of Bridge and Structural Engineers), Helsinki, 1988.

15

Modifying existing bridges with minimum traffic disruption: *adjacent widening and on-line span increase*

15.1. Introduction
15.2. Underbridge modification
15.3. Overbridge modification
15.4. References

Fig. 15.1. Modifying over-bridge for widening D3M to D4M

15.1. Introduction

The UK road-widening programme recently announced by the Department of Transport (DTp) envisages the spending of some £1500 million over ten years on the associated bridge widening, lengthening and replacement. Unlike bridge-building for new roads or motorways on virtually greenfield sites, a common situation over the past four decades, the new bridge modifications or replacements will have to be built in the presence of traffic which is already heavy enough to require the widening of the road or motorway carried or traversed.

Notional costs can be attributed to the traffic delays caused by roadworks. On some heavily trafficked sections of a dual three-lane motorway (D3M), weekly costs of £200 000 to provide a 2 + 2 contraflow would not be unusual. It is not surprising, therefore, that traffic disruption costs during bridge modification or replacement can well exceed the cost of a completely new bridge.

For this reason the DTp is encouraging the use of fast methods, keeping extra traffic disruption to the minimum, for bridge modification or replacement arising from road widening. The word extra is emphasised because the road-widening process itself requires extensive traffic disruption and it would indeed be beneficial if the bridge operations could be undertaken within the disruption times required by the local road-widening operation.

Faced with a trunk road or motorway widening, the choice for the original bridges will lie between modification of the existing structure or demolition and replacement.

In the case of modification, it is possible to save any extra disruption to the road widening while causing minimum disruption to the road carried or crossed. This is obviously more desirable and generally more economic than demolition and replacement, which requires

(a) either the erection of a temporary bridge off-line, or the temporary closure of the side road
(b) demolition of the original bridge after any necessary diversion of services
(c) the building of a replacement bridge
(d) removal of any temporary bridge after diversion of services into the replacement bridge.

All these operations require careful planning.

As with bridge strengthening, bridge modification and replacement during road widening require innovative techniques to avoid too much traffic disruption. With a considerable variety of existing bridge stock, there will be few standard solutions, and most bridge modification or replacement operations will require individual treatment. However, many of the basic design and construction principles can be formulated and some of the possible techniques listed. The following sections, 15.2 and 15.3, covering modification, and chapter 16, covering replacement, provide an introduction to this new challenge of the 1990s to the bridge engineer.

15.2. Underbridge modification

Most trunk road or motorway underbridges incorporate pedestrian footpaths or hard shoulders at the outer edges, a feature which can offer considerable assistance in any widening of the road carried.

In the case of underbridges on a motorway requiring widening, the hard shoulders can provide the extra lanes with no need for bridge widening, presuming that the loss of hard shoulders can be accepted over a short length of motorway. This was indeed the solution for the M62 lane widening on Rakewood Viaduct, described in section 12.6. Nevertheless, some bridge strengthening may be required, as with Rakewood, and devised similarly to minimise traffic disruption, if any, to the major road carried or any road crossed.

Where such a procedure is not possible and bridge widening is required, the hard shoulders or pedestrian walkways can be temporarily closed to form useful working areas during widening.

Symmetric underbridge widening, generally an extension repeat of the original bridge, can be constructed for most of the time independently of and with no traffic disruption to the main deck by leaving a narrow stitch joint between the new and old constructions. The completion work can be undertaken within the untrafficked footpath or hard shoulder and the new widening, with the old parapets demolished, services moved into the widening, and transverse stitch reinforcement drilled into the existing deck before the stitch joint is concreted. American research has shown that traffic-induced vibrations during concrete bridge repair and widening are not detrimental provided that the concrete used is low slump and the new reinforcement is securely fixed.[1]

Most underbridges carry the major road over a minor road, and traffic disruption on the minor road, if any, can usually be limited to short periods of one-way light-controlled traffic operation.

In the fortunately less frequent cases where the underbridge carrying a major road crosses another major road, widening operations will be further

Fig. 15.2. Overbridge modification procedures for widening D3M to D4M

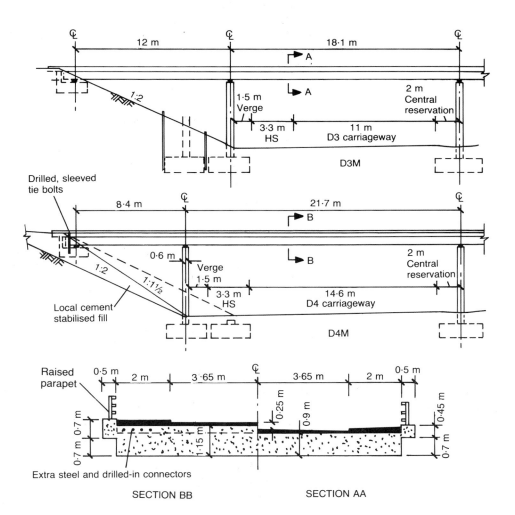

restricted by the need to minimise traffic disruption both below and on the bridge. In this case the very severe traffic restrictions might dictate an entirely different method of construction for the underbridge widening. Where the original deck is of in situ concrete construction, precast concrete or steel composite construction might be needed for the widening to minimise traffic disruption underneath. Some ingenuity will then be required in the transverse stitching of the differing new and old constructions.

Where viaduct widenings are required over major roads, resort might be required to the cantilever methods of construction described in chapter 4.

15.3. Overbridge modification

The effect of trunk road or motorway widening on existing overbridges requires that the single or twin spans over the carriageways be increased and, possibly, the bridge length also (Fig. 15.1).

Avoiding traffic disruption on the motorway or trunk road crossed is a much more difficult proposition than the underbridge widening described in section 15.2. However, in some cases, modifications of certain types of existing overbridge can permit retention in a strengthened state with little, if any, associated traffic disruption to the underlying road widening.

A typical case is shown in Fig. 15.2, where a square four-span continuous in situ reinforced concrete slab bridge carrying a two-lane minor road over a D3M is to be modified to suit a symmetrical extra lane widening to a D4M. The original twin 18·1 m motorway spans require increase to twin 21·7 m spans. However, the bridge length can be maintained by reducing the end spans from the original 12 m over 1 : 2 embankment slopes to 8·4 m over locally increased 1 : 1½ embankment slopes using cement-stabilised fill.

The construction would follow the listed stages

(a) construction of new verge piers and foundations in sheeted excavation in the existing embankment slopes up to the soffit of the existing deck; addition of interlinked jacking between bearings

(b) closure of one lane and footway on the minor road and institution of one-way working controlled by traffic lights, with a temporary central crash barrier; diversion of any services

(c) removal of surfacing and parapet behind a temporary shield on half deck, scarification of top of existing concrete, drilling-in of steel shear connectors/links, fixing of new top reinforcement, addition of concrete to increase parapet and deck depth by 250–300 mm

(d) replacement of diverted services, parapet and surfacing; repetition of operation on the second half of the deck

(e) fixing of sleeved tie-down bolts under footway at ends of deck to suit uplift safety factors by drilling and grouting into bankseat

(f) jacking-up of deck at new verge piers to remove load at old verge piers, measured by strain and feeler gauges located at old bearings

(g) removal of old piers by concrete-sawing within verge safety barrier

(h) jacking down of deck on to grouted new verge pier bearings

(i) construction of new 1 : 1½ cement-stabilised slopes over existing embankment front slope; building up of approach embankment to match 250–300 mm increase in deck depth.

The extra bending moments and pier reactions created are shown for the case of a typical uniformly distributed load in Fig. 15.3. The bending moment increases of up to 50% and shears of up to 20% are catered for by the increased deck depth and new reinforcement. The extra load on the central pier is less than 20%, which generally could be accommodated by considering the increased concrete strength due to the accumulated age when the new

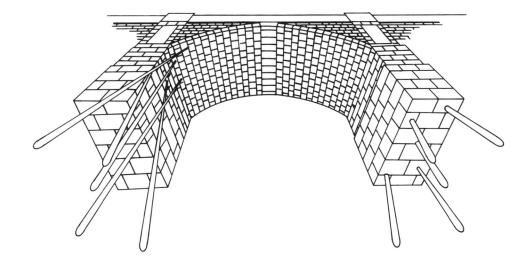

Fig. 15.3. Overbridge typical bending changes for widening D3M to D4M (w is weight of concrete per unit volume)

loading is added. Clause 303 of the old BS 114 (1957) permitted an increase of 24% for concrete no more than twelve months old at loading.

The increase in soil loading might be more difficult to accommodate for a tight original design, although the soil could have been strengthened by years of consolidation under the original bridge loading.

In the unlikely event of a requirement to strengthen the central pier foundation, resort could be made to Messrs Fondedile's Pali Radice piling[2] (Fig. 15.4). These concrete piles with casing diameter 140–220 mm could be installed by drilling through the deck central pier and original foundation, giving piles with capacities of 350–750 kN.

In the event that the pier stem also needed strengthening, extra reinforcement could be grouted into the pier holes drilled for the piling below. The mobile drilling rigs, as small as 1 m by 2 m in plan area, could be located over the pier within the alternating half-deck working areas. The operation would not interfere with the motorway traffic below, although careful procedures would be required to contain the water used in the drilling operations.

Further improvements to the procedure could lie in using lightweight concrete for the increased deck depth and dispensing with the drilled-in shear connectors. Tests on new concrete added to old concrete beams with and without shear connectors indicated little difference in composite behaviour.[3]

Even more attractive in some cases would be the possibility of undertaking the overbridge widening in advance of the motorway widening at a time when the minor-road resurfacing falls due. It is also possible that the top surface of the overbridge will have suffered salt penetration and some reinforcement

Fig. 15.4. Pali Radice piling

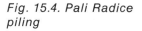

corrosion, revealed during the scarifying of the concrete. A careful engineer would then ensure that the new top reinforcement is epoxy-coated and that the new bridge waterproofing is of the sprayed-on variety, as described in chapter 11.

15.4. References

1. HARSH and DARWIN. Traffic-induced vibrations and bridge repairs. *Concrete International*, 1986, May.
2. ATTWOOD. Pale Radice: their uses in stabilising existing retaining walls (bridges). *Ground Engng*, 1987, Oct.
3. CLARKE. *Tests on composite beams for W.S. Atkins & Partners.* Cement and Concrete Association, Research & Development Division, Wexham Springs, 1976.

16

Bridge replacement with minimum traffic disruption: *lifting or rotating preformed decks into place*

16.1. Introduction
16.2. Steel–concrete composite decks
16.3. Steel–concrete prestressed composite decks
16.4. Prestressed concrete decks
16.5. References

Fig. 16.1. Maupré Valley viaduct, Charolles, France

16.1. Introduction

Possibly the majority of underbridges can be modified for road widening as indicated in the previous chapter. However, only a small number of overbridges will be suitable for the modifications indicated in that chapter. Most will require demolition, a temporary bridge off-line and replacement on-line.

For bridge replacements the Department of Transport (DTp) is encouraging the use of single spans across the widened trunk road or motorway to avoid the extra traffic disruption created by building a new central reservation pier. This represents a change from the original requirements for new motorway bridges, where central reservation piers were generally mandatory to reduce spans and costs, unless bend sightlines were impeded.

To avoid the costs of extra traffic disruption associated with building a new central reservation pier, and yet avoid the greater single span across the widened road, it might be possible to retain an original central reservation pier for cases of symmetric motorway widening only. The greater loadings imposed by the longer spans of the replacement deck would be accommodated as described in section 15.3, with the extra piling undertaken by drilling from the top of the replacement deck before traffic occupation.

In the event that the original central pier cannot be retained or indeed that the original bridge had a single motorway or trunk road span with no central pier, then the replacement bridge will require to cross the main road in one span.

The increase in construction depth with be considerable, particularly when a four-span bridge crossing a dual three-lane motorway (D3M) is replaced with a new bridge crossing a D4M. The main-span requirement for a square bridge changes from approximately 18 m to 43–45 m, depending on pier or abutment support, representing an increase in construction depth of at least a metre for a three-span continuous replacement deck and even more for a simply supported single span. If the original bridge crossed with minimum headroom clearance then the replacement bridge will require the local raising of the side road profile by at least a metre. This means additional approach earthworks and land acquisition, adding further to the already considerable cost of the replacement bridge.

However, using the principles described in chapter 3, the depth of a three-span continuous deck or a single simply supported span can be varied to produce a depth reduction at the ends to minimise the extra earthworks and land acquisition required for the new approach embankments.

As shown in Fig. 16.2, illustrating a three-span or single-span square bridge crossing a normal-crossfall D4M, an end deck depth reduction can be obtained by using a three-span sucker deck. Even larger reductions in earthworks can be gained by curving the side road profile to produce a curved uniform depth or a reversed fishbelly, variable depth, single span deck. The deck depth saving possible compared with the level uniform depth deck shown is the 0·5 m D4M crossfall for the sucker deck and however much can be gained within sightline limitations by curving the side road profile, usually no more than 0·5 m. For the $2\frac{1}{2}$: 1 side slopes shown, the curved profile of the single span deck results in a 4% grade on the approach roads between wing walls, representing a further saving in the length and end height of the wing walls and earthworks.

In general, the badly matched side and main spans, together with the large uplift forces at the bankseats, do not favour continuous three-span arrangements, except perhaps where good rock is available for bankseat anchorage. Single spans and abutment supports are usually preferred, even allowing for the greater depth of construction required. The choice between the reversed fishbelly and uniform depth curved single spans (the latter taking advantage of the D4M crossfall) depends on relative costs and aesthetic preference.

The new verge piers, bankseats and side spans, or abutments and wing walls, can generally be built with no traffic disruption. However, the main road span deck, with minimum spans of 36 m for D2M to D3M widening and 43 m for D3M to D4M widening, will require some traffic disruptions extra to those caused by road widening during construction. To minimise these disruptions, generally during short night-time possessions or lane diversions of the trunk road or motorway, the following desirable features should be considered during replacement bridge design.

(a) A single span plus abutments avoids the excessive uplift of three-span solutions.

(b) Minimum-weight solutions mean less heavy mobile cranage for lifting into position.

(c) Beams and deck slabs should preferably be preformed off-site and transported to site in manageable sizes. This generally means maximum lengths of 27·5 m and widths of 4·5 m to satisfy DTp requirements for minimum-disruption road transportation.

(d) An area for assembly and storage is required on site to store and make up the beams to full span length from the shorter transported elements and for storage of the slab elements.

(e) In situ concrete work over the road widening should generally be limited to grouting of prestressing and concreting of stitch joints. Suitable shields will be required to prevent material spills on to the road beneath. However, multi-stage composite concrete construction may be considered where minimum-weight precast elements can be erected over the road widening and in situ concrete added in the safe confines of a trough girder or on top of precast concrete slabs or structurally participating steel formwork.

Some solutions fulfilling some of these desirable features are described in sections 16.2–16.4.

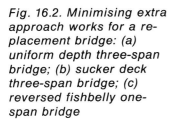

Fig. 16.2. Minimising extra approach works for a replacement bridge: (a) uniform depth three-span bridge; (b) sucker deck three-span bridge; (c) reversed fishbelly one-span bridge

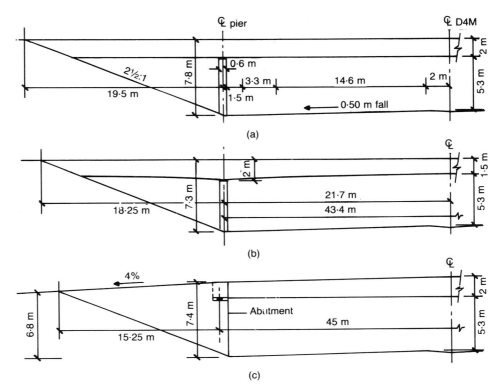

16.2. Steel–concrete composite decks

Fig. 16.3. Composite steel beam/precast concrete deck 45 m replacement bridge

The minimum approximate 37 m and 44 m spans of the main beams for single-span D3M or D4M replacements tend to favour steel construction. Steel beams can be brought to site in braced pairs in readily transportable sections up to the 27·5 m long and 4·5 m wide limits. On site they can be friction-grip-bolted to full span length prior to lifting into place. A typical solution for a two-lane side road crossing is the single 45 m span devised by Hayward and Sadler,[1] with a commendable construction depth of only 1·89 m, shown in Fig. 16.3. The full-width deck slabs are precast in short lengths and placed over the three previously erected steel-beam assemblies, pockets in the slabs fitting over clusters of shear connection welded studs. Stitch joints between slabs are merely filled with in situ concrete, the stitch being unreinforced.

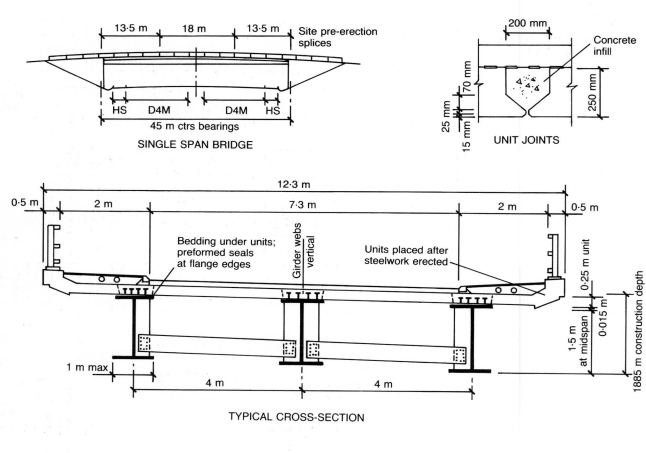

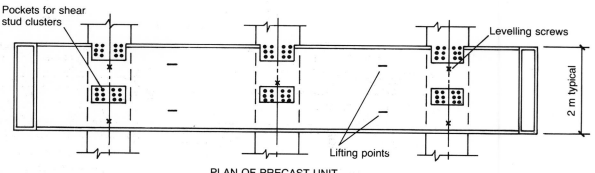

It is suggested that the procedure could be improved further by fixing the shear studs through the pockets after slab placement. This would permit a push-out assembly of the slab units from one or both ends of the bridge, with no disruptive lifting into place by cranes from the widened road.

Another improvement would lie in the provision for future maintenance painting with minimum, if any, traffic disruption. This could be accommodated by using GRP or aluminium enclosures or by providing a painting gantry, adding 200–300 mm to the required construction depth.

A possible weakness of the deck slab stitch joint shown is that differential temperature and wheel load effects could cause joint cracking. If the waterproofing is good enough, the cracking could be accepted. A more positive approach would be to provide wider precast slab units with lapped or coupler-

Fig. 16.4. Assembly and stitch jointing for precast concrete deck slabs

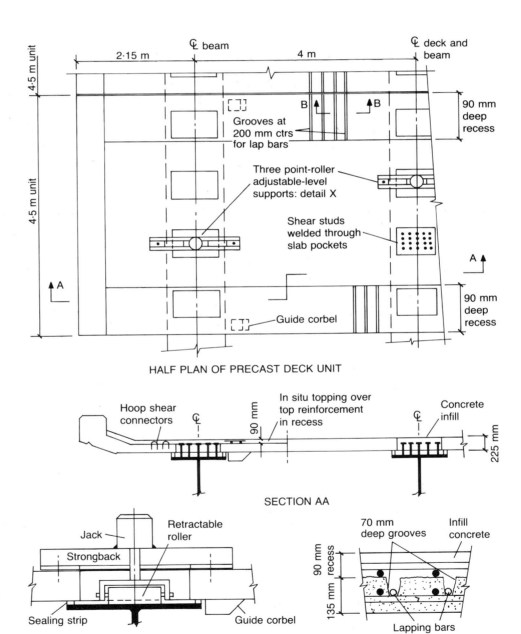

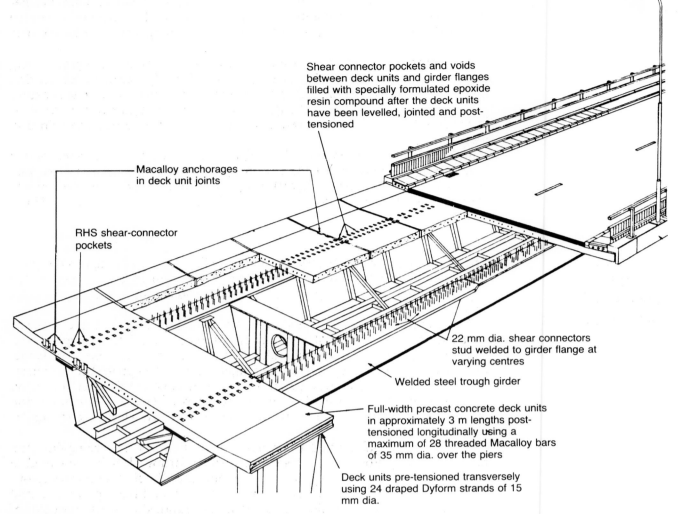

Shear connector pockets and voids between deck units and girder flanges filled with specially formulated epoxide resin compound after the deck units have been levelled, jointed and post-tensioned

Macalloy anchorages in deck unit joints

RHS shear-connector pockets

22 mm dia. shear connectors stud welded to girder flange at varying centres

Welded steel trough girder

Full-width precast concrete deck units in approximately 3 m lengths post-tensioned longitudinally using a maximum of 28 threaded Macalloy bars of 35 mm dia. over the piers

Deck units pre-tensioned transversely using 24 draped Dyform strands of 15 mm dia.

Fig. 16.5. Fully prestressed precast concrete deck slabs

Fig. 16.6. Cross-section of Maupré Valley viaduct

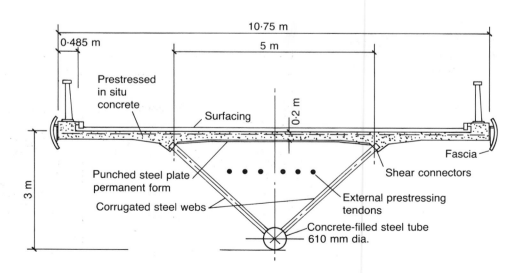

10·75 m

0·485 m

5 m

Prestressed in situ concrete

Surfacing

0·2 m

3 m

Fascia

Punched steel plate permanent form

Shear connectors

Corrugated steel webs

External prestressing tendons

Concrete-filled steel tube 610 mm dia.

connected longitudinal reinforcement. Fig. 16.4 shows a lapped joint alternative using in situ topping composite with a dished length of precast slab in the lap locations. The push-out roller bearing and levelling jacks assembly is also shown.

Even more elaborate ideas, using longitudinal and transverse prestressing to provide crack-free deck slabs, were proposed for a flyover in North London in the late 1960s[2] (Fig. 16.5). It is doubtful whether such expensive measures would be applicable today, although the longitudinal and transverse prestressing of in situ deck slabs has been used recently to advantage, as described in section 16.3.

It has been suggested that the weight and connection problems of the concrete slabs be dispensed with by building all-steel decks consisting of steel box girders supporting orthotropic steel plate decks. Assembly would probably be from half-width sections and making extensive use of HSFG bolting.

16.3. Steel–concrete prestressed composite decks

The 325 m long Maupré Valley viaduct near Charolles in France was designed and built by Campenon Bernard BTP[3] in the mid-1980s as part of the highways innovative policy of the French Administration for Roads (Fig. 16.1).

The highly original cross-section is shown in Fig. 16.6. It is a composite construction of structural steel and prestressed concrete. The triangular box, 3 m deep, consists of a concrete-filled 610 mm dia. steel tube bottom flange, twin inclined webs of trapezoidally corrugated 8 mm steel plate shear-connected to a closing transversely prestressed in situ concrete deck slab cast on participating permanent perforated steel formwork. The whole cross-section is longitudinally prestressed by external cables deflected within the triangular girder.

The structure was erected using push-out techniques, the triangular steel beam section of tube, webs and steel permanent formwork being delivered to site in transportable 12 m sections for assembly into the six consecutive spans, maximum 53·6 m. The steel section was pushed out and the top slab cast and prestressed in close succession, a procedure encouraged by the low weight of under 8 t per metre of the 11 m wide deck.

This highly innovative type of hybrid construction could well be used as an alternative to the steel composite proposal of Fig. 16.3. It would not normally be built in push-out fashion for reasons of access, economy and safety, but

Fig. 16.7. Composite steel beam/prestressed in situ concrete deck 45 m replacement bridge

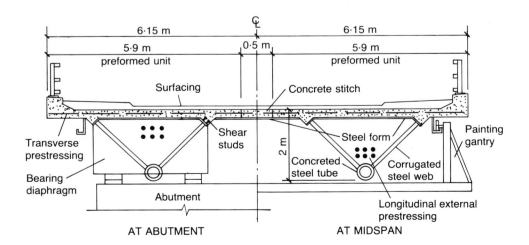

lifted into place as with the design shown in Fig. 16.3. Fig. 16.7 shows the proposal, which uses smaller twin versions of the Maupré cross-section erected side by side, with a slab stitch joint formed with either reinforcement or coupled tendons. Initial sizings indicate a total lift of under 200 t for each of the two half-decks.

The smaller girder depth is high enough to allow access to the prestressing cable and for interior painting inspection and maintenance. An exterior painting gantry is also indicated, adding 200 mm to the effective construction depth. It is proposed that the gantry should be stored in an off-site maintenance compound and hoisted into position from the verges. Alternatively, the construction could be enclosed in GRP or aluminium, although this could add extra expense and detract from the novel and attractive appearance.

Another innovative method comes from Belgium[4] and adds prestressed composite beam prestressing to the pre-bent Preflex bridge beam used in the UK in the 1960s and 1970s. The new beam is shown in Fig. 16.8 and consists of a pre-bent steel beam encased in hybrid prestressed concrete.

The highly complex assembly consists of the following stages. First, the steel beams are placed on a pre-tensioning bed and are prestressed by wires (a) attached to the bottom flange. Second, the prestressed steel beam is preflexed (i.e. bent downwards) by external jacks. Next the pre-tensioning strands (b) are stressed by the pre-tensioning bed jacks. Then the beam and associated prestressing strands and cables are concreted and cured. Next the

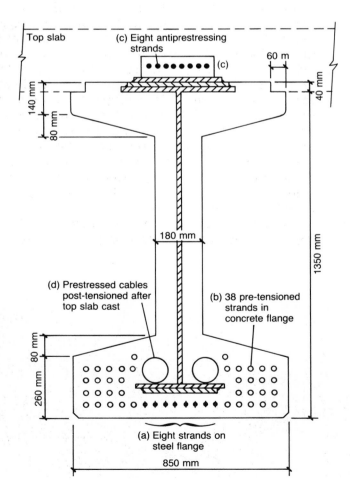

Fig. 16.8. Prestressed and preflexed steel–concrete composite beam: span 47 m, weight 90 t; overall depth 1·6 m

antiprestressing strands (c) attached to the top flange and outside the concrete are prestressed. Then the preflex loading of the second stage is removed by release of the external jacks. Following this, the pre-tensioning is released on to the composite beam. Next the beams are transported to site and erected; the formwork for the top slab reinforced concrete is hung from the beams. Then the antiprestressing strands (c) are released and removed. Next, the top reinforced concrete slab is cast and finally the post-tensioning cables (d) are prestressed.

The beams were used for a viaduct crossing the River Meuse near Liège in Belgium, with spans of 47 m. A remarkably low construction depth of 1·55 mm, giving a span/depth ratio of 31, demonstrated the high strength of these complex beams and their possible suitability for replacement bridges in the UK.

Unless special transport arrangements were possible, it would be necessary to bring the steel beams in sections for assembly by site welding. All the deflection and prestressing beds and equipment would also have to be site-based. No doubt this could be accepted where a large number of replacement bridges would justify the setting-up of a central site adjacent to the motorway for beam production.

16.4. Prestressed concrete decks

Precast pre-tensioned concrete bridge beams available in the current ranges are not long enough for even the 36 m minimum D2M to D3M widening requirement. Larger standard I beams were available in the UK in the 1970s and are currently available in America. However, in February 1992 the UK Prestressed Concrete Association launched a bigger version of the Y beam —the super Y beam. This is suitable for bridges of up to 40 m span. No doubt this will be stretched even further in the future to cater for 45 m spans and D4M widening. Larger beams would still cause transportation problems, as they would be in excess of the 27·5 m DTp limit. Undoubtedly, a precast concrete beam similar in principle to those described in chapter 6 could provide a good solution. The beams would be assembled on site by post-tensioning of two or three readily transportable factory-precast segments, in this case reinforced rather than pretensioned.

Until such solutions become available from the Prestressed Concrete Association, who recently provided UK engineers with the Y beam, it seems regrettable that some of the advantages of prestressed concrete cannot be added for replacement decks.

Possible alternative solutions could be with the multi-staging principle demonstrated by the prestressed preflexed beams described in section 16.3.

Fig. 16.9. M63 River Mersey bridges, Manchester

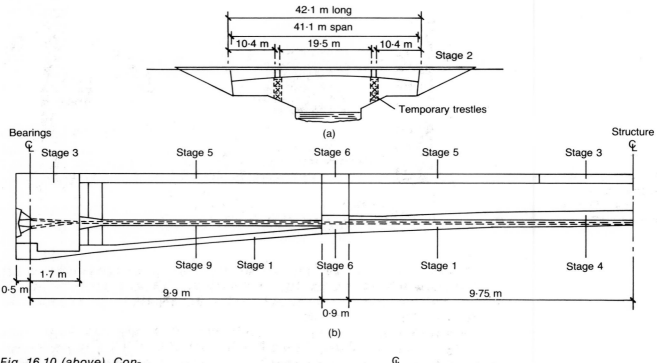

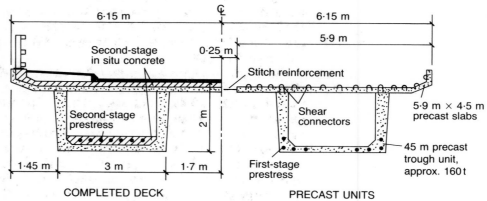

Fig. 16.10 (above). Construction stages for decks of Mersey bridges: (a) elevation; (b) longitudinal section of girder

Fig. 16.11 (right). Prestressed concrete 45 m replacement bridge

Fig. 16.12 (below). Drawbridge viaduct construction

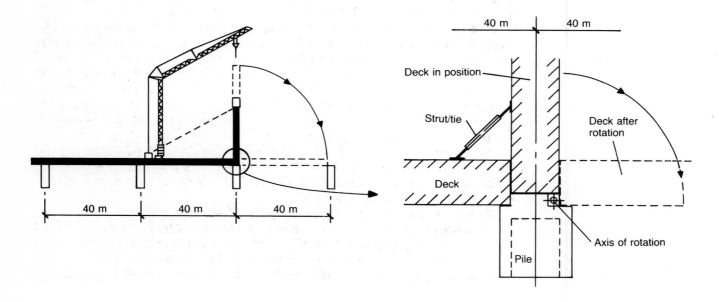

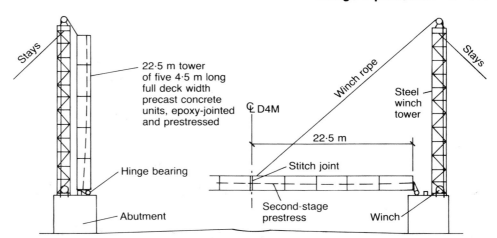

Fig. 16.13. Prestressed segmental precast concrete 45 m replacement bridge

The principle is basically to use low-weight first-stage elements for easier erection, and to add second-stage composite strengthening up to the limit of the weight acceptable to the first-stage elements. The sequence is repeated for as many stages as are required.

An early demonstration of this principle was on two 41 m single span bridges across the Mersey,[5] completed in 1974 (Fig. 16.9). Two prestressed concrete trough beams composite with a reinforced concrete deck slab were used on each of the 16·5 m wide bridges. For aesthetic reasons only, the prestressed trough beams had curved soffits, with a construction depth of 1·83 m at midspan.

The beam construction is shown in Fig. 16.10, with the multi-stage construction as follows. In stage 1, the central section, length 19·5 m, and the end sections, length 10·4 m each, are precast, and three 19·5 m long tendons in the central section are stressed and grouted. In stage 2, the self-supporting units are hoisted on to the abutments and temporary trestles, with a 0·9 m splice gap between. Stage 3 consists of adding in situ end blocks and part of the length of the top flange. In stage 4, in situ concrete thickening is added to the bottom flange in the central segment. In stage 5, the remaining lengths of the in situ top flange are cast. In stage 6, the in situ infill splice joint is cast. Stage 7 consists of stressing, and then grouting only over the central segment, the eight 42·1 m long tendons; box girders now span between the abutments and the temporary trestles are removed. Stage 8 consists of casting the remaining deck slab between and outside the box girders. Stage 9 consists of casting in situ the intermediate slab around eight stressed cables and four ducted unstressed cables in the end segment. In stage 10, the remaining four 42·1 m long tendons are stressed and grouted. In stage 11, the parapet beams are cast.

The procedure could be adapted to provide a prestressed trough beam alternative for the bridge constructed as a single steel–concrete composite span of 45 m shown in Fig. 16.3. The proposal is shown in Fig. 16.11.

Prestressed concrete could also be used for another form of erection, the 'drawbridge' method, which also comes from Continental Europe. The idea is based on the Argentobel arch bridge built in Germany, and a French proposal for multi-span viaducts.[6]

Figure 16.12 shows the original proposal. The in situ concrete box girder is built vertically over temporary hinges on one abutment using slipforming techniques and external prestressing. The tower crane used for concreting is stayed for the vertical rotation into place of the completed deck.

This method, originally proposed for multi-span construction, would only prove viable for the construction of a number of similar replacement bridges, where the large and expensive erection equipment could have an economical number of uses. If this was possible, the use of double-leaf drawbridge construction could be considered, with only half-span construction heights required over each abutment. A small stitching gap at midspan could be coupled or reinforced and concreted after rotation, with further composite concrete and external prestressing added to cater for surfacing and live loading.

With the reduced height of the drawbridge leaves, it could also be possible to substitute full-width prestressed precast concrete segmental construction. These various proposals are shown in Fig. 16.13 as an alternative to the 45 m span replacement bridge shown in Figs 16.3, 16.7 and 16.11.

16.5. References

1. HAYWARD and SADLER. Bridge replacement for the bridge widening. Construction Marketing Symposium on Bridge Replacement, Leamington Spa, 1991.
2. BROWN *et al*. Hendon Urban Motorway—Fiveways Interchange. Institutions of Highway and Structural Engineers, London, August 1971.
3. CAUSSE and DUVIARD. Maupré Viaduct near Charolles—a bridge deck with corrugated steel plate webs constructed by the incremental launching technique. International Association of Bridge and Structural Engineers Symposium, Concrete Structures for the Future, Paris, 1987.
4. BELFROID-RONVEAX. Composite pre-bent prestressed beam for bridges and buildings. International Association of Bridge and Structural Engineers Symposium, Concrete Structures for the Future, Paris, 1987.
5. PRITCHARD. Concrete is final choice for M63 Mersey bridges. *Concrete Mag.*, 1974, July.
6. MATHIVAT. The recent evolution of prestressed concrete bridges. International Association of Bridge and Structural Engineers Symposium, Concrete Structures for the Future, Paris, 1987.